*Power Pattern Offenses
for Winning Basketball*

Power Pattern Offenses for Winning Basketball

Jack Nagle

Parker Publishing Company
West Nyack, New York

© 1986 by

PARKER PUBLISHING COMPANY, INC.

West Nyack, N.Y.

Library of Congress Cataloging-in-Publication Data

Nagle, Jack, date
  Power pattern offenses for winning basketball.

  Includes index.
  1. Basketball—Offense. 2. Basketball—Coaching.
I. Title.
GV889.N34 1986   796.32′32   85-32072
ISBN 0-13-687708-7

PRINTED IN THE UNITED STATES OF AMERICA

I dedicate this book to

the young men and women who have played for me;

the loyal and capable assistant coaches who have served with me;

coaches Fred "Tex" Winter, Pete Newell, and the late John Benington who shared their great knowledge with me in the "early days";

Harold Rose and Dr. Lawrence Grant, principals of Whitefish Bay High School, for their faith in me and for their guidance;

Stan Albeck of the Chicago Bulls, John Weinert of Bowling Green University and Rick Sund of the Dallas Mavericks for their friendship;

Al McGuire, Hank Raymonds, Rick Majerus, Bob Weingart and Betsy Van Sickle of Marquette University and Jim Mott of the University of Wisconsin for their cooperation and support;

my three sons, Chuck, Bill and Jim, who have never failed me;

my wife, Maudie, who believes in me regardless of the final score;

and to "Honshu" wherever you are!

Foreword

Jack Nagle is not only a winning basketball coach, he is also one of the most innovative manipulators of the X's and O's in the annals of the game. Rival coaches say that to observe Jack Nagle's team in action is to witness a basketball clinic "in the flesh." The fact that his tactics are widely copied by fellow coaches is a flattering testimony to the effectiveness of the power pattern approach to basketball offense. Jack's teaching techniques have made him a featured basketball clinician throughout the United States. His informative basketball articles in various coaching journals have helped many a "struggling" coach solve his problems.

Coach Nagle's contributions to the great game of basketball have afforded him a place as a Charter Member in the Wisconsin Basketball Coaches Hall of Fame. This book, then, is a reflection of Jack Nagle's many years of experience as a highly successful high school and college coach and as a professional scout for the National Basketball Association.

I enthusiastically endorse *Power Pattern Offenses for Winning Basketball* as a sound and sensible teaching tool for basketball coaches of men's and women's teams on all levels of competition. Such a book is long overdue.

Al McGuire

Head Basketball Coach
Marquette University
1964–1977

How This Book Can Help You Install a Powerful Offense

I scored my first field goal at the age of eight—on the dusty playground behind the Creswell Elementary School in Shreveport, Louisiana—and I have been in love with the game of basketball ever since.

After graduation from Marquette University and following a four-year stint in the U.S. Air Corps during World War II, I began my coaching career as assistant basketball coach at my alma mater. Those were the days of early masters of basketball coaching: Adolph Rupp of Kentucky, Pete Newell of California, Hank Iba of Oklahoma A & M, "Phog" Allen of Kansas, Bruce Drake of Oklahoma, "Tex" Winter of Kansas State, Jack Gardner of Utah, and "Doc" Carlson of Pittsburgh—among others.

As assistant coach and chief scout at Marquette, I had the great fortune to observe the teams of these legendary coaches. Each of these basketball pioneers had his own original offensive style. In fact, each was known for his specific pattern offense: Adolph Rupp's Continuity Pattern; Pete Newell's Reverse Action; Hank Iba's Controlled Passing Game; "Phog" Allen's Post Isolation Series; "Tex" Winter's Triple Post; Jack Gardner's Post Interchange Continuity; and "Doc" Carlson's Figure Eight.

The offensive styles of these basketball innovators and the precision with which their teams performed them have had a profound and lasting effect on my coaching philosophy. In short, I believe in pattern basketball!

Then, too, many of the refreshing ideas of the modern-day giants of the college and professional game—Dean Smith, Bobby Knight, Denny Crum, Stan Albeck, Hubie Brown and Dick Motta—to name only a few, have been included in the development of the power pattern continuities.

In addition, the associations I have enjoyed with coaches of high school men's and women's teams have further solid-ified my faith in pattern basketball.

The professional game in particular has added an impor-tant dimension to my offensive philosophy. As a scout for the Cleveland Cavaliers and presently for the Dallas Mavericks of the National Basketball Association, I have observed the ef-fective "quick-action" patterns used by NBA teams—patterns which have been expressly designed to "beat" the 24-second clock. Many of these "quickie" techniques have also been "transfused" into the power pattern attacks.

The power patterns in this book represent a piecing to-gether of the best ideas of the old and the new. The patterns have produced perennial winners on all levels of play and with both men's and women's teams. The best testimonial to the effectiveness of the power pattern offense is the fact that many coaches throughout the United States and in foreign countries have adopted the patterns totally or in part.

Should there be those among you who believe that pattern basketball is old-fashioned or out-of-date, nothing could be further from the truth! Thumb through coaching magazines, attend basketball clinics, observe college and professional teams in person or on TV, and you will discover that pattern bas-ketball is alive and well! Even the professional teams, blessed with the greatest one-on-one performers in the world, fre-quently rely on patterns to "set them free"!

During those seasons when we were short on talent—and there have been many—we have produced winning teams by utilizing pattern continuities that emphasized the strengths and minimized the weaknesses of the available personnel.

The time-limiting restrictions of a "shot clock" do not

minimize the effectiveness of the power pattern continuities in the slightest. *In fact, we discovered that our patterns more often produced a good shot quicker than did a free-lance style of play!* It is a matter of record that the "shot clock" teams that have implemented our patterns have experienced no problems in obtaining the high-percentage shot before the time limit expires.

Coaches of high school girls' and collegiate women's teams will find that the material in the following chapters is entirely appropriate on all levels of play. I have used the pattern approach with high school girls for the past twelve years, during which we have compiled an 89 percent victory record!

The advocate of motion and flex offenses, as well as passing game enthusiasts, will discover that the power patterns provide plenty of "motion," sufficient "flex," and ample "pass, cut, and screen" plays.

Most important, the "change of side" continuities used in all power pattern attacks afford weakside player movement, a minimum of resetting, and counterplays which make predetermined defensive coverage very difficult. Moreover, each power pattern incorporates those options that are most difficult to defend.

The power patterns can be adapted to all tempos of play. They can be used with the fast break and as "early offense" attacks. Stall and delay games are included in the package.

The power patterns detailed in this book differ from most pattern offenses in that they provide for a variety of initial entry maneuvers which defy defensive anticipation.

A significant aspect of the power pattern offenses is that while each ball handler is "set up" either by the initial entry option or the swing continuity, he is allowed the freedom to pass, drive or shoot as dictated by the defense! While the power patterns generally require predetermined movements, they not only provide freedom of opportunity but emphatically encourage it!

For those coaches who are probing for effective methods of combating conventional zones, changing or alternating defenses, match-up and combination zones, and man-to-man tactics, rest assured that there is plenty of game-tested material to aid you in solving your problems.

The chapter dealing with sideline, endline, jump-ball, and delay patterns will provide your team with many bonus baskets.

If you are searching for a new "wrinkle" to incorporate into your own "pet" system you will find many original ideas from which to choose.

If full-court presses have proved troublesome, I am certain that the adjustable stack attack will do the job for you as it has for so many other coaches.

I am confident that those coaches who are addicted to the fast-breaking style of play will be pleased with the innovative ideas presented in Chapter 1, "Fast Breaking the Defenses with the Early Offense Transition Pattern."

The various patterns are fortified with basket cuts, shuffle options, double screens, backdoor plays, up picks, down picks, and baseline blocks. The techniques of "begging for the ball," "fanning out," and "mini-flashing" are completely explained and diagramed. Each power pattern continuity is designed to keep the help side of the defense occupied, thereby assuring adequate "operating room" for the ball-side options.

Power Pattern Offenses for Winning Basketball explains the systems of play that have been my bread and butter! You will find no personal anecdotes; no rehashing of great victories; no tidbits of nostalgia with which to pad the pages. You *will* discover sound, sensible, and successful systems of pattern play—systems that are largely responsible for the longevity I have enjoyed in the wonderfully exciting, but very demanding, profession of basketball coaching.

Jack Nagle

Contents

1

Fast Breaking
the Defenses with
the Early Offense
Transition Pattern

FAST-BREAK PHILOSOPHY

We are confirmed believers in fast-break transition basketball. However, as with each of our power pattern attacks, our early offense patterns stress controlled player movement and specific attack routes.

We also are convinced that while speed is desirable, *control* is even more important. Our motto is "speed, but controlled speed!" As a matter of fact, our most successful fast-breaking teams consisted of players who possessed only average speed. These teams were successful because they rebounded well; made the quick, accurate outlet pass; filled the lanes rapidly; expertly executed the pass and the dribble; and observed the rules of action.

In developing the early offense pattern, we borrowed a page from the playbooks of the National Basketball Association (NBA) teams. Since the NBA teams must shoot the basketball within a 24-second time limit, they usually advance the ball quickly, looking for the fast-break lay-up or a short jump shot. If the shot is not there, the players set up their "early offense"— a predetermined series of options designed to produce a high-percentage shot. This system is becoming increasingly popular with both men's and women's teams on all levels of play.

Our version of this transition game is based on utilizing the available personnel to maximum advantage by numbering each position and assigning definite routes and responsibilities to each player according to his particular capabilities. In addition, our early offense transition pattern is designed to be initiated from each of the various zone and man-to-man defenses and from defensive rebounds, interceptions, made and missed free throw attempts, and following opponent's field goals. We also originate the fast-break offense from midcourt jump-ball formations. This phase of the attack is discussed in Chapter 9, "Scoring Easy Baskets with the Endline, Sideline, Jump-Ball, and Delay Power Patterns."

DUTIES AND CAPABILITIES OF PLAYERS

Players 1 and 2 are the guards. They play the defensive frontline positions, and each must be capable of performing the usual middle man and wing fundamentals during the primary three-man break attack. Each must be well-versed in playing the two-man game, which is explained later in this chapter.

Player 3 is usually the small forward. However, the best choice for this position is a good back-line defender and rebounder whose primary responsibility is to fill the open wing during the primary advance. He must be capable of setting a good screen. He is also required to play a role in the two-man game.

Players 4 and 5 have similar duties. They *always trail* during the three-man break attack. Both should be excellent rebounders and good passers. If one or both can shoot the 15–17 footer from the side of the key, the attack is even more powerful.

Coaching Point: The rules are simple and easily learned: Players 4 and 5 always trail; 1 and 2 always fill the middle or an open wing, depending on the positioning of each at the moment when the ball is secured; player 3 always fills an open wing with one exception (see Diagram 1-4b). Drills and various practice procedures ensure proper understanding and execution of the rules and routes.

THE THREE PHASES OF THE
EARLY OFFENSE TRANSITION PATTERN

The early offense consists of three distinct phases: the Go phase, which is the primary three-man break attack; Swing It, which is the secondary or trailer series; and Set It, which is the third and final stage of the action.

Initiating the Go Phase
(Three-Man Attack)

Initially, we teach the various phases of the early offense by employing the one-man front defenses (1-2-2 and 1-3-1). Diagram 1-1 illustrates the 1-2-2 zone, a perfect springboard for the Go attack because each player is stationed in the exact position that he will occupy in the fast-break advance.

Go Routes and Options

When the ball is rebounded or a steal occurs, the first option is 1's advancement of the ball down the middle with 2 and 3 filling the wings and 4 and 5 trailing the advance. The wings must sprint to a position approximately six feet ahead of the middle man, splitting the distance between the sideline and the outside edge of the foul lane. If the middle man cannot advance all the way, he stops in the outer half of the foul circle and pulls up for a jump shot or a pass to either wing, who cuts toward the basket at a 45-degree angle from the foul line extended (Diagram 1-2).

If the middle man is not in control on the downcourt thrust, either wing dribbles down the sideline, reads the defense, and reacts accordingly.

Of course, the Go attack is nothing more than the standard three-man, fast-break pattern that many teams employ. However, it was not until we installed our numbering system and

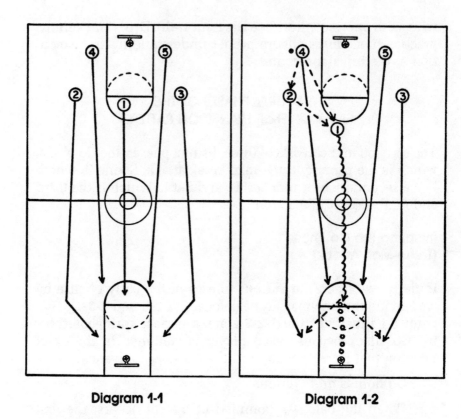

Diagram 1-1   Diagram 1-2

perfected the necessary techniques that we were able to beat the defense down the floor and obtain the high-percentage shot more consistently.

Coaching Point: With the ball at a wing or baseline position, the 1-2-2 alignment shifts to a 2-3 or 2-1-2 formation. However, the Go routes of all defenders remain constant since player 1 is always in a front-middle position. The same advantage is present when using the 1-3-1 zone defense.

*Initiating the Go Phase
from the Two-Man Front-Zone Defenses*

When initiating the Go phase from a 2-1-2 or 2-3 zone defensive set, a slight adjustment is necessary in order to route

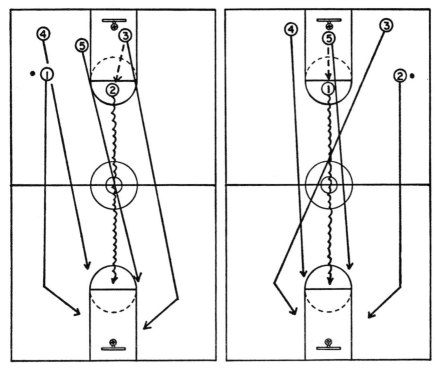

Diagram 1-3a   Diagram 1-3b

player 3 to the open wing. Usually either player 1 or player 2 will be forced to cover an offensive wing as the other front-line defender drops to the foul-line area. When this overload occurs on the side away from back-line defender 3, the route positioning is ideal (Diagram 1-3a).

On the other hand, when the overload is on 3's side of the court, he must fill the weakside wing since 1 and 2 are already in perfect position to fill their lanes (Diagram 1-3b).

Coaching Point: The adjustment shown in Diagram 1-3b is a simple one and is easily learned in practice situations. Since 2 is covering the wing, it is 1's responsibility to fill the middle lane on the fast break. Notice also the straight-line cut to the open wing by 3. To "loop" or "angle" into position would drastically slow the formation of the frontal attack.

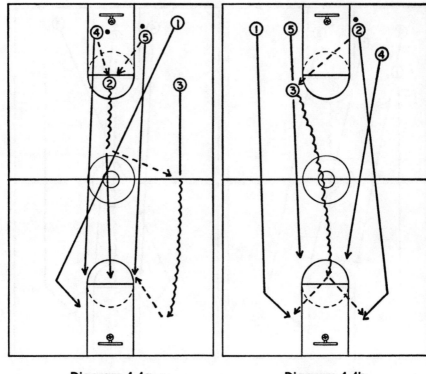

Diagram 1-4a   Diagram 1-4b

Forming the Go Attack
from the Man-to-Man Defenses

When the transition is attempted from a man-to-man defense, forming the Go attack is sometimes difficult, especially
if either 1 or 2 (or both) is covering his man on or near the
baseline. In such an eventuality, the standard rule is to break
either 1, 2, or 3 (whoever is in the best position to do so) into
the middle area with the remaining "breakers" filling the open
lanes (Diagrams 1-4a and 1-4b).

Coaching Point: Emphasize to your players that whenever
they find themselves in an awkward position, *they must not
force the play.* They must discontinue the fast-break attempt,
move downcourt under control, and set up the halfcourt of-

fense. Practice situations will clear up any problems with player routes when initiating the Go attack from the man-to-man defense.

Note: Initial positioning and rules of coverage for the various zone defenses frequently vary from one coach to another. All will agree, however, that the defense is the catapult from which a successful fast-break attack springs. A successful fast-break attack depends on proper player placement, definite area responsibility, effective rebound positioning, and primary and secondary outlet options.

Initiating Swing It
(Secondary Attack)

When the Go phase fails to produce the desired result, the secondary attack options (Swing It) are implemented without delay. If the wing is in control of the ball, he immediately passes to the trailer or to a wing and the continuity begins.

The First Swing Routes and Options

Diagram 1-5 illustrates the first swing of the continuity. Player 2, the right wing, is in control. He picks up his dribble, pivots, and passes to trailer 4. If 4 is open and in range, he may shoot. If not, 4 passes to trailer 5, who may shoot if open

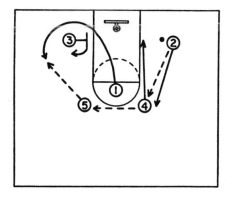

Diagram 1-5

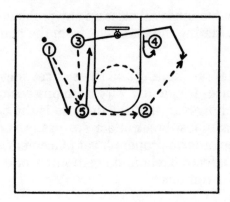

Diagram 1-6

and in range. If 5 elects not to shoot, he passes to 1, who has timed his cut off 3's baseline screen. Player 1 has a number of options: He can shoot, drive solo, drive off a rear screen set by 3, and execute a pick-and-roll play as 3 rolls to the hoop. In addition, 1 and 3 can play the two-man game by working together—passing and return passing, posting up and maneuvering for a shot, and so on.

Notice that after 4 passes to 5, he interchanges with 2, thereby affording a stronger rebound alignment without jeopardizing the defensive balance.

Second Swing Routes and Options

If no shot is available after a complete first swing, the second and final swing begins as player 1 (or 3) passes to 5. The *second swing options* are similar to those of the first swing. You will notice, however, that 3 now uses 4's screen and 5 exchanges with 1 for rebounding purposes. Players 3 and 4 explore the same options as previously described for players 1 and 3 (Diagram 1-6).

Coaching Point: Should the middle man initiate the action by passing to a trailer, he makes the normal cut down the lane and "hooks" around the weakside screen as usual. This optional pass by 1 triggers the first swing. Notice the interchange by 5 and 3 (Diagram 1-7a). If no shot results, the completion

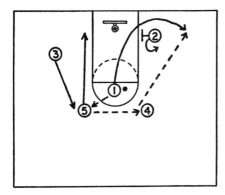
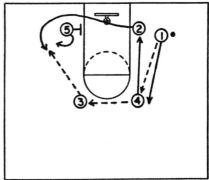

Diagram 1-7a   Diagram 1-7b

of the second swing occurs, as illustrated in Diagram 1-7b. Player 1 passes back to 4, 4 passes to 3 and interchanges with 1, and 3 hits 2 coming off 5's screen, and so on.

The early offense patterns have now been completed. The rebounders, 4 and 5, are repositioned under the basket and the perimeter players are outside, ready to initiate the final phase—Set It.

Coaching Point: Since swinging the ball is vital to the success of the secondary phase, the defense will attempt to disrupt the perimeter ball movement by denying the passing lanes, particularly from the wing to trailer and from trailer to trailer. Two adjustments will defeat these denial stunts.

The Wing-to-Trailer Denial Adjustment

The wing-to-trailer denial adjustment is easily accomplished. Wing man 2 in possession of the ball pivots, 1 clears around the weakside screen as usual, and 4 backdoors the overplaying X4. Player 5 replaces 4 and 1 replaces 5. Both 5 and 1 are now in position to swing the ball if necessary (Diagram 1-8).

If the inside defense is not alert, 4 is frequently open. However, if 4 is not open for the pass from 2, 2 relays to 5 and the swing continues with 4 replacing 1 behind 3's screen (Diagram 1-9).

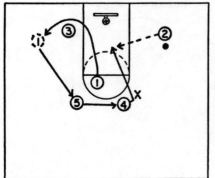

Diagram 1-8

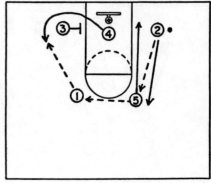

Diagram 1-9

The Trailer-to-Trailer Denial Adjustment

Another productive adjustment is made on the trailer-to-trailer denial. In Diagram 1-10, X5 denies the passing lane from 4 to 5, 4 executes a skip pass to 1 on the baseline, and 1 exercises the options detailed earlier. If 1 is covered, 3 flashes to the ball for a pass and a quick jumper. Players 3, 4, and 5 rebound, and 1 joins 2 at the top of the circle as *safeties* (Diagram 1-11).

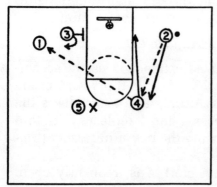

Diagram 1-10

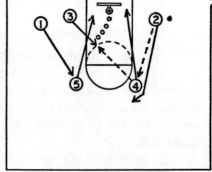

Diagram 1-11

Initiating the Third Phase
(Set It)

Set It is exactly what the term implies. Since our two-swing motion in the Swing It phase consists of an interchange by each player, the defense is readily identified as zone or man-to-man. The point guard calls the appropriate halfcourt offense and we flow into the attack. We include this phase as part of our early offense merely to alert the players to the fact that it is time to realign appropriately and begin one of the halfcourt patterns detailed in the following chapters.

INITIATING THE EARLY OFFENSE
FROM SPECIAL SITUATIONS

Successful Free-Throw Attempts

As shown in Diagram 1-12, player 5 inbounds to 2, who has moved to the ball side from his initial position at the top of the foul circle. Player 1 takes the middle route, and 3, after screening the shooter, cuts down the weak side. Players 4 and 5 trail as usual. When the defense attempts to deny the pass to 2, 1 delays his cut down the middle, maneuvers to receive the inbounds pass, and proceeds with the pattern. Since we rarely score on the primary phase due to precautionary defensive alignments by the shooting team, we enjoy excellent success by employing the Swing It attack every time down the court.

     Coaching Point: If the defense puts on a tough full-court press and you have difficulty inbounding or advancing the ball, abandon this tactic and set up the adjustable stack attack, which is explained in Chapter 2.

Unsuccessful Free-Throw Attempts

While we seldom score on the primary phase following a made foul shot, the Go phase works successfully after rebounding a

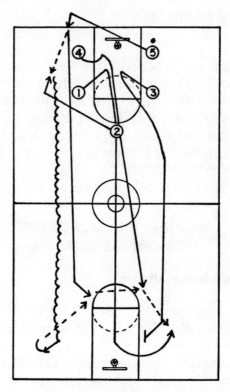

Diagram 1-12

missed shot, particularly if the opponent stations only one player as safety. The alignment and the routes are exactly the same as detailed in Diagram 1-12. We screen off the boards, grab the rebound, outlet the ball and *"Go!"* Of course, we will go into our Swing It, if necessary.

Successful Field-Goal Attempts

The early offense following a successful field-goal attempt observes the same basic rules. The attack begins as player 4 or 5 (the better inbounder) takes the ball out of the net, sprints to an out-of-bounds position, and passes to 2 or 3. Player 1 cuts to the middle area and expects the inbounds pass if 2 and

3 are unable to free themselves. The remaining wing fills the weakside lane as always, and the attack is underway. Players 4 and 5 trail the play.

   Coaching Point: The inbounder must not turn and throw. He must be sure that the passing lanes are open before he passes. In addition, should the opponent employ a full-court press, discretion must be used in attempting this tactic. The rule of thumb when facing a pressure defense early in the game is to attack quickly a couple of times, and if you are successful, continue to do so. When facing severe full-court man-to-man pressure, encourage the inbounder to "run the baseline" following successful field goals and free throws. If you do not succeed with these tactics, set up the adjustable stack attack.

Steals, Interceptions, and Long Rebounds

The procedure for fast breaking following steals and interceptions is learned easily. If the steal or interception occurs in the back line of defense, you proceed in the same manner as if it were a short rebound. If possession is secured by a front-line defender, release a player (or players) who is in a favorable position to beat the defenders downcourt, and throw the lead pass. You do not want the interceptor to dribble in this situation since the pass is more efficient. Regard the long rebound into the foul-line area as an interception and play it in the same manner.

DRILLS FOR BUILDING
THE EARLY OFFENSE TRANSITION PATTERN

Since the success of the early offense transition pattern depends on the proper execution of offensive fundamentals, emphasis must be placed on the usual "standard" drills to perfect lay-ups, jump shots, pivoting, dribbling, and so on. The familiar three-player full-court drills also are essential to the improvement of ball handling, and passing and dribbling "on the run."

In addition to these teaching-tool staples there are four special drills that have proved to be invaluable in teaching the Early Offense.

Three-on-Three Multipurpose Transition Drill

Select three defensive players who will wear blue shirts. Half the remaining squad members (wearing white shirts) take a position behind one endline, and the remaining half behind the other endline. Three whites come out and play offense against the blues, who are the defenders. They play three-on-three basketball until the defense gains control by rebounding, stealing, or intercepting. The blues now initiate the fast-break Go pattern and must score on the transition. No halfcourt setup is allowed to the blues. At this point, three new whites assume the offense, the same blues remain on defense, and the drill continues. Change the blues after three trips down the court.

This drill gives every player (including those who are usually trailers) the opportunity to practice the full-court skills necessary not only to the transition game but also the backcourt pressure offense. Furthermore, the whites are working on screens, give and goes, pick and rolls, offensive rebounding, outlet prevention, and dribbler containment. The blues are practicing defensive techniques as well as the transition skills. This is our favorite drill and the players truly enjoy it!

Five-on-Zero Controlled Transition Drill

The entire squad forms behind the baseline. Five players enter the court and assume their normal positions in the defense specified by the coach. The coach calls the pattern and the option, "shoots" the ball at the backboard and the players rebound and run the pattern called for. For example, the coach may call: "Go, middle shoot!" This programs the players to assume their normal routes and advance the ball into the front court with the middle man taking the shot. Another call might be "Swing It, wing control, 'hooker' shoot." This signals a complete first swing of the ball from the wing to the trailers to the middle man, who has "hooked" around the baseline screen for a pass and a shot. If the coach calls "Second swing, Set It, overload," the players respond by executing two complete reversals (swings) with no shot, after which they set it up in the overload and wing-swing pattern, as detailed in Chapter 3.

The coach also "passes" to a defender and yells "Interception!" and the players react according to the basic rules for interceptions. The transition game is also set up from free-throw setups and successful field-goal attempts.

When one group has completed their pattern, they sprint back and take their place on the endline as the next group enters the court for action.

In this drill, it is wise to program a few patterns from each defensive set, repeating the pattern with each new group. As with any drill of this type, there are so many options that the coach must write the patterns and options in his daily practice plan so that he can "rattle them off" confidently and maintain a record of the options that have been covered and those that have not. Review the explanations in this chapter and compile a checklist of all possible options for ready reference.

Finally, make your calls slowly and distinctly. Remember that when the players are learning, their minds need time to register what has just been learned.

The Five-On-Five
Controlled Transition Scrimmage Drill

Use this drill only after the players have mastered the routes and options as practiced in the five-on-zero controlled transition drill.

The first team aligns in a specified defense. The second team is on offense and plays to score. The defense, upon gaining control, will activate the transition game, using only the Go and the Swing It phases. Following a score or loss of ball by the transition team, both teams reset, turn around, and go again. The first team remains on defense until changed by the coach.

A very important aspect of this drill is the occasional "programming" of the second team defenders. The coach huddles with them and instructs as follows: "This time, overplay the trailer-to-trailer pass"; or "Next time they swing it, overplay the second trailer"; or "When the wing pivots in to pass to the trailer, deny the ball to the trailer"; and so on. This method aids the transition team by affording them the opportunity to react and defeat these defensive tactics. The defensive team is also learning "denial" techniques.

Change the defensive sets often, since you must be prepared to initiate the early offense from any formation.

The "Blow 'Em Out" Drill

This drill is a confidence builder in which the early offense team goes "full tilt" with control, of course, using all phases of the attack and including the Set It Up phase. *Do not stop the play for coaching comments!* Incorporate all tactics: changing defenses, free-throw setups, successful field-goal attempts, and versus full- and halfcourt defenses. Again, all ten players are learning something.

The coach makes substitutions and calls the defensive changes from the sidelines, simulating game conditions. The managers referee and "call them close."

After a specified period of time (usually twenty minutes), time-out is called and the coach critiques the performance. The weak points are discussed, and a short drill period is devoted to correcting them.

SUMMARY

Most coaches will agree that fast-break transition basketball is the most difficult game for coaches to teach and for players to learn to do well. Pure perfection even for superior players is virtually impossible. However, while we do "mess it up" once in a while, we have great confidence in our early offense transition pattern!

Each phase is based on sound principles; each phase is

teachable as a separate unit; each phase smoothly blends with the next to form a compact package.

When installing the secondary-attack phase of the transition game with an inexperienced squad, it is wise to include only the first "swing" options both in practice and in early season contests. Only after you are satisfied that your players have mastered the first "swing" continuity should you add the second "swing" options.

The coach who decides to tackle the arduous task of installing an early offense attack must be willing to spend long hours on the practice court; he must demand the utmost in physical condition from his players; and, above all, he must have the patience of Job!

Once you have included the early offense transition game in your arsenal of basketball weaponry, you not only will have something well worth working for, you also will have something very special!

2

Destroying the
Backcourt Presses with
the Adjustable Stack Attack

HOW THE TRIPLE STACK
IDENTIFIES THE DEFENSES

One of the most perplexing questions to be answered when
facing backcourt pressure occurs when the basketball is ready
to be put into play by the inbounder—is the defense employing
a zone or man-to-man press? The development of the adjustable stack attack climaxed a long search for an attack formation
that would not only enable the players to identify quickly the
type of defense but would also provide instant adjustments of
the initial set to ensure the safe inbounding of the ball and the
effective advancement versus the various types of zone presses,
straight man-to-man pressure, and combinations thereof.

The midcourt triple-stack alignment enables each player
to positively identify the defensive set. The three basic press
alignments—man-to-man, 1-2-1-1 zone, and 2-2-1 zone—are
shown in Diagrams 2-1, 2-2, and 2-3, respectively.

Since players 1, 3, 4, and 5 are in a perfect position to
observe the defensive formation, they are ready to react accordingly. Player 2 must take a quick look at the position of
the defenders before he faces the inbounder. If the defense is
guarding each player one on one, the players employ the man-
to-man tactics. If the defense shows a zone alignment, zone-
press principles are used.

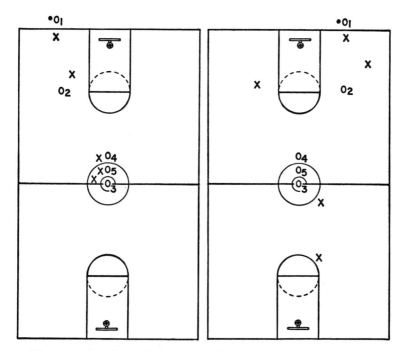

Diagram 2-1 (Man-to-Man)   **Diagram 2-2 (1-2-1-1 Zone)**

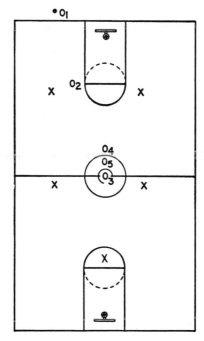

Diagram 2-3 (2-2-1 Zone)

Coaching Point: Many coaches advocate rapid inbounding versus all types of full-court pressure. In other words, "Get it in and go before the defense can set!" However, we have never been completely satisfied with the "quickie" method of putting the ball in play. It has been our experience that we can adjust the attack more intelligently when we are fully aware of the nature of the defense before putting the ball in play.

DUTIES AND CAPABILITIES OF EACH POSITION

Player 1 is the inbounder. He must be an excellent passer, as he must deliver the basketball to the proper receiver at the proper time and to the right place. He must be a capable dribbler as he is frequently required to advance the ball. Peripheral vision is absolutely essential because in many instances four teammates will be breaking to four predetermined spots. In addition, player 1 must be adept at relaying the ball to an open teammate during the downcourt advance. He always inbounds from outside the foul lane to ensure that the backboard or net will not interfere with his inbounds pass. After the inbounds pass is completed, *he must step in directly behind the ball.*

Coaching Point: Many press attacks are *one-side* oriented. The players are coached to inbound the ball from the same side of the court when the choice is theirs following a successful field goal or free throw. This "same side" inbounding allows the pressing team to position their defensive specialists—trappers, interceptors, one-on-one experts, and so on—in the most advantageous spots. The practice of varying the inbounding side has proved to be successful in causing occasional setup problems for the defenders.

Player 2 aligns near the elbow on the same side of the court as 1. He must take a quick look at the defensive alignment before facing the inbounder. He must be a capable dribbler, passer, and ball handler, and must possess good change-of-direction moves, particularly when maneuvering to free himself for the initial inbounds pass. A tall guard who possesses these skills is ideal for the 2 position.

Player 3 sets in the last spot in the midcourt triple stack, directly behind 5, and must be ready to sprint to the side of the court opposite 2. Ideally, he should possess the same skills as 2, since he will be required to adjust to 2's position on occasion.

Player 4, the front player in the triple stack, is ideally a tall forward who can catch a high, hard pass from the in-bounder or from any teammate as the ball advances. His initial move is always dictated by the nature of the defensive set. This player should be chosen carefully. He should be a capable scorer from the baseline as he is a primary scoring target as the ball advances into the front court. It is important that player 4 positions himself in a direct line with the ball as it is advanced.

Player 5 is a post-type player. He stations himself in the middle position in the stack. When the ball is ready to be put in play, he takes two or three quick angle steps to the side away from the inbounder and then cuts to the backcourt foul-lane area to serve as a possible pass receiver. He must be adept at feeding the wings (players 2 and 3) as they break down the sidelines. Upon receiving the pass, he must turn, face his at-tackers, and observe the positions of the defenders as well as the positions of his teammates. If player 4 is open downcourt, a pass to him is the first option. If he is able to advance the ball on the dribble, he does so. In short, player 5 reads the defense and reacts to it.

Diagram 2-4 shows the basic routes of the players from the initial triple stack formation.

Coaching Point: Players 2, 3, 4, and 5 must "run through the ball" when receiving the inbounds pass. ("Running though the ball" is our term for meeting and receiving the pass on the run. To stop running before receiving the ball is to invite a steal or deflection by a defender.) In addition, the passer must deliver the ball to the side away from the defender, and the

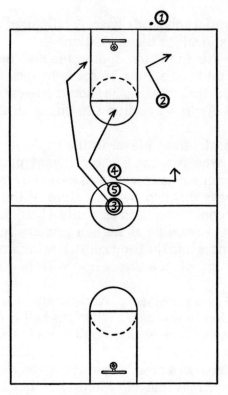

Diagram 2-4

receiver must present a hand target on his open side. We stress catching the ball with one hand and then pulling it in to a two-hand, under-the-chin position. We also insist that the elbows be spread at right angles to the body as the ball is held under the chin. This technique ensures that the ball is protected from swarming, arm-flailing defenders.

RULES OF ACTION VERSUS BACKCOURT PRESSURE

1. After a score by the opponent, players 3, 4, and 5 must *sprint* to the midcourt attack positions. Player 1 delays slightly before taking the ball out-of-bounds in order

to allow time for the formation to set and to observe the defense. Player 2 sets at the elbow and faces the inbounder.

2. Player 1 must vary the side of the court from which he inbounds. This variation does not affect the position of the midcourt stack.

3. The basic midcourt stack alignment is as follows: player 4 in the first spot, player 5 in the middle, and player 3 in the third position at the backcourt edge of the center restraining circle. (See Diagram 2-4.)

4. Players 2, 3, 4, and 5 begin their cuts at the exact moment that 1 faces them from out-of-bounds. (To signal the start of the action with the customary slap of the ball or by calling "break" wastes time and is not permitted.)

5. All players must react simultaneously as follows:

   a. Player 2 maneuvers to free himself for a possible pass from player 1. He does his faking and cutting on his side of the court only. This ensures that the cutting lanes to the ball by the other players will not be obstructed.

   b. Player 3 cuts to the baseline-sideline spot on the side away from player 2. He maneuvers for a possible pass.

   c. Player 5 breaks to the foul lane area, looking for a pass.

   d. Player 4 holds his position at the front of the stack as a partial screen for players 3 and 5. Immediately after they have cut away, player 4 must move to a midcourt position directly ahead of the ball as the ball is being inbounded. He maintains his position ahead of the ball as the ball advances. He is a primary target in the downcourt advance and is often open for a scoring pass. (See Diagram 2-5.)

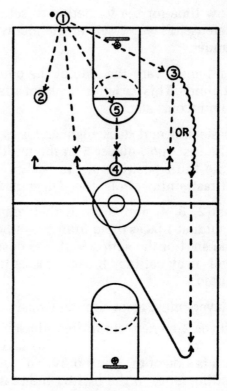

Diagram 2-5

ATTACKING THE 1-2-1-1 BACKCOURT ZONE PRESS

When the attack begins, *player 1 has four immediate passing options:* to player 2 on the strong side; to player 3 on the weak side; to player 5 in the foul lane area; or to player 4 who has cut directly in front of the ball in the midcourt area. (See Diagram 2-6.)

The most effective option is the long pass to 4, because this option completely defeats the team whose purpose it is to allow the short pass to 2 and immediately trap him in the deep backcourt. When the pass to player 4 is successful, he turns, faces the front court, observes the defensive positioning,

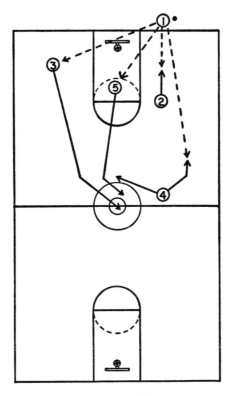

Diagram 2-6

and reacts. If he can beat a midcourt defender on the dribble, he does so. If not, he looks for player 5 coming down the middle, player 1 or 2 who is trailing, or player 3 sprinting down the weakside sideline. (See Diagram 2-7.)

Should player 5 receive the inbounds pass, player 1 steps in behind the ball, players 2 and 3 assume the wing positions, and player 4, following the rule, positions himself ahead of the ball. The formation now resembles a 1-3-1 set. Player 5 protects the ball, turns to face the enemy, and passes to an open teammate (Diagram 2-8).

A pass to a wing often results in either an "open-lane" dribble toward the front court and a pass to 4 for a short jump

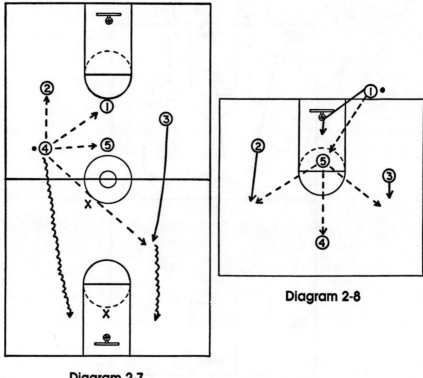

Diagram 2-8

Diagram 2-7

shot from the baseline, or a direct pass from the wing to 4, who maneuvers for a shot. Both options are shown in Diagram 2-9.

If 4 receives 5's pass at midcourt, he becomes the middle man in the *three-man break attack*, with 2 and 3 filling the wings and 1 and 5 trailing. This attack pattern is fully explained in Chapter 1, "Fast Breaking the Defenses with the Early Offense Transition Pattern." (See Diagram 2-10.)

In the unlikely event that 5 cannot pass to the wings or to 4, he returns the ball to 1 who is trailing.

We prefer not to make the initial pass to 2 because this is what the defense hopes to accomplish. When 2 is in control, defenders X1 and X2 will join in a trap on 2, and X3 will

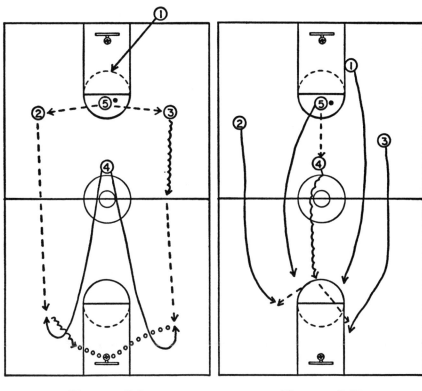

Diagram 2-9   Diagram 2-10

attempt to cut the lead to 1 while X4 covers 4. Player 2 does not fight the trap nor does he attempt a pass to 5 or to 3. Instead, he immediately returns the ball to 1 who has stepped in behind the ball, and 1 relays to 3 or 5. (See Diagram 2-11.)

If 5 receives the pass, the options are the same as described in Diagram 2-8. If 3 receives from either 1 or from 5, he is usually open for a speed dribble toward the front court where 4, ahead of the ball, may be open for a pass and a shot. (See Diagram 2-12.)

If 3 is stopped, he passes back to 1, 1 relays to 2, and 2 drives into the front court. Naturally, every action by the offense must be crisp and quick because the ball must be advanced into the front court before the ten-second time limit

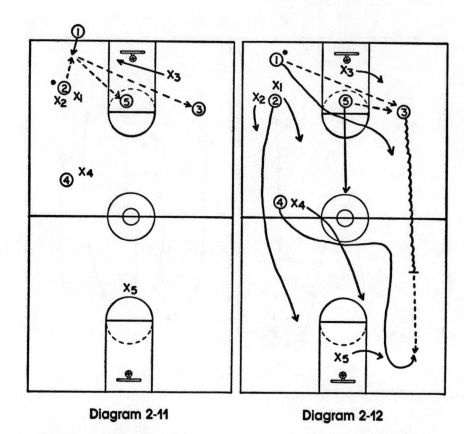

Diagram 2-11   **Diagram 2-12**

expires. Frequently, once the ball is reversed and relayed to
the weakside wing, the lane into the front court is wide open
because the defense has initially overshifted to the ball side.

Coaching Point: The practice of having the inbounder step
in *directly behind the ball* is important not only to provide
relief for a trapped player but also to prevent a third defender
from cutting off the passing lane to 1. Should the inbounder
move into the court at an "angle," a quick defender can move
to a denial position between the trapped player and the inbounder. (See Diagrams 2-13 and 2-14.)

In addition, since the inbounder must have ample room
to move into, it is imperative that you drill the receivers to
"get open" as far from the baseline as possible. Finally, player

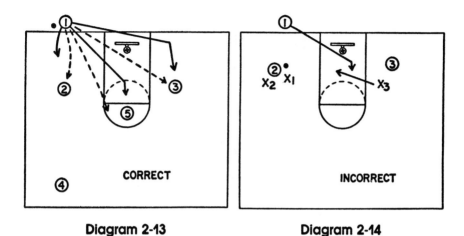

| Diagram 2-13 | Diagram 2-14 |

1 always trails the advance to relieve a trap at any position in the backcourt.

DEFEATING THE 2-2-1 BACKCOURT ZONE PRESSES

The 2-2-1 backcourt presses are of two types, the *three-quarter court alignment* and the *full-court set*. Regardless of the initial formation, the 2-2-1 presses usually are geared toward the same primary objective: to force the ball (preferably on the dribble) down the sideline and form a trap near the midcourt line. The adjustable stack attack easily defeats this tactical objective.

Attacking the Three-Quarter Court 2-2-1

The three-quarter court version of the 2-2-1 allows the ball to be inbounded without pressure. The strongside front defender then will attempt to force the dribbler down the sideline to a point at which the strongside back player joins him in forming a trap on the ball handler. The weakside defenders will move to denial positions to prevent an escape pass out of the trap.

The Three-Man Front Adjustment

In attacking this defense, we make a slight adjustment in the downcourt advance, while maintaining our basic forma-

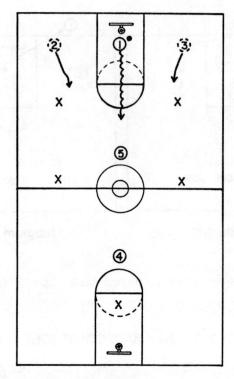

Diagram 2-15

tion. The ball is inbounded to 2, who immediately returns the pass to 1 stepping in behind the ball. Player 3 breaks to his usual weakside wing area, but 5 holds at his initial position and 4 moves to the front-court foul circle. Players 2, 1, and 3 form a three-man front with the ball in the middle and the wings approximately three feet to the rear of the line of the ball. (See Diagram 2-15.)

The Three-man Break Attack

At this point, we read the defensive adjustment and react accordingly. Should the two front defenders trap 1 in the middle, he has the option of passing back to either wing or to 5 near midcourt. The latter is our preferred choice since this pass sets up the three-man break attack: 5 hits 4 in the front

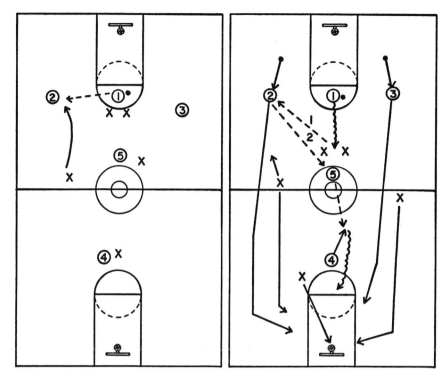

Diagram 2-16 *(Incorrect)*   **Diagram 2-17 *(Correct)***

court, and the wings sprint down the sidelines for the three-on-one opportunity.

    Coaching Point: Positioning the spread wings to the rear of the line of the ball makes it impractical for the rear-line defenders to attempt a pinch-off the passing lanes from the middle man to either wing. If the wings were to move *ahead* of the middle man, the pass from the middle to the wing would have to be made over the top of the trap—a most dangerous pass. (See Diagrams 2-16 and 2-17.)

Attacking the Full-Court 2-2-1

The Decoy Maneuvers

    Unlike the three-quarter court press, the full-court 2-2-1 attempts to deny the inbounds pass. As the front defender

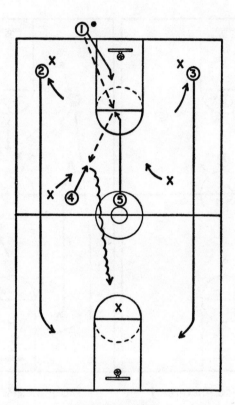

Diagram 2-18

covering player 2 works to deny the pass, 2 spreads to the near sideline, taking the defender with him. Player 3 cuts into his normal weakside area, also acting as a decoy. These decoying maneuvers by 2 and 3 clear the middle for 5, who breaks into the lane area and receives the uncontested pass from 1. Player 5 turns and hits 4, who moves into an open gap, and players 2 and 3 stream down the sidelines, forming the three-man break attack (Diagram 2-18).

After scoring one or two quick lay-ups or short jump shots, the defense will invariably discontinue this form of pressure.

Coaching Point: The baseline pass to player 4 on our downcourt advance and the three-man break attack are our most productive scoring options against backcourt zone press defenses. However, we do not "force" these plays. We prefer to play patiently and do what it takes to advance the ball into the front court. We will attack to score only if the opportunity is of the high-percentage variety. We spend many hours of practice time perfecting our halfcourt patterns, and we have confidence in them as scoring machines. To attempt "free-lance" gambles is contrary to our offensive philosophy.

THE SPREAD ADJUSTMENT
VERSUS MAN-TO-MAN PRESSURE

As shown in Diagram 2-1, the defensive set initially identifies the man-to-man press since each defender is matched one-on-one with an offensive player. Of course, the defense might very well use a man-to-man defense only to switch to some form of zone pressure as the ball is inbounded. If this "switching" tactic continues, stay in the regular adjustable stack attack, since it is as effective in handling man-to-man pressure as it is in defeating the zone presses.

However, should you wish to vary the attack versus the man-to-man defense, another simple adjustment may be made. This variation is called the "spread."

The beginning set is the same as usual; however, instead of moving the triple-stack players to their normal positions, we instruct them to spread along the midcourt line as soon as the ball is inbounded to player 2. (See Diagram 2-19.)

Coaching Point: Player 2's starting position at the elbow will afford him ample area to maneuver to receive the inbounds pass. As he runs straight toward the inbounder, he will be able to create an open passing lane no matter how severe the overplay by the defender. If the defender is overplaying the left, player 2 cuts to the right; if the overplay is to the right, he veers to the left. Should the defensive player "front him all the way," player 2 stops short, reverses his direction, and receives a lob pass from player 1. (See Diagrams 2-20a and 2-20b.)

Upon receiving the ball, player 2 faces the defender and

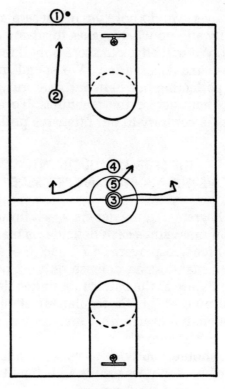

Diagram 2-19

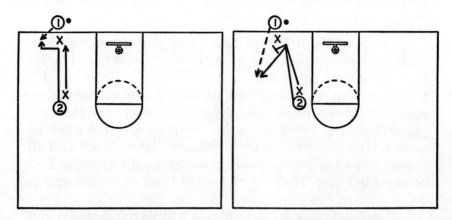

Diagram 2-20a   **Diagram 2-20b**

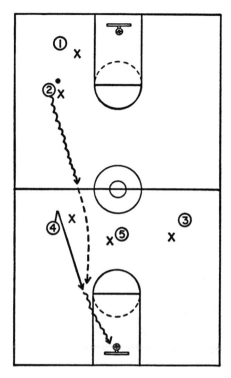

Diagram 2-21a

player 1 steps in behind as usual. *If defenders X1 and X2 join to trap 2, 2 returns the ball to 1, who quickly dribbles away from the trap, and 2 trails.*

Players 3, 4, and 5 observe the progress of the dribbler and move into the front court, *maintaining the spread formation.*The spreaders are constantly on the alert for signs of approaching trouble on the part of the dribbler and break to the ball to rescue him when necessary.

The dribbler keeps his head up as he advances, always looking for an open teammate ahead of him. Should any spreader be severely fronted, the dribbler may pick up the dribble and deliver a backdoor pass to the overplayed player for a lay-up. (See Diagram 2-21a.)

After safely advancing the ball into the front court, the players immediately set up a halfcourt pattern.

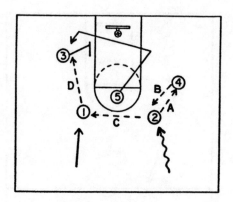

Diagram 2-21b

Completing the Spread Attack
with the Early Offense Swing Option

The spread attack rarely produces a fast-break score. On the other hand, we particularly like to finish the spread attack with a variation of the early offense swing phase. In Diagram 2-21b, for example, as player 2 dribbles into the front court, he calls "Swing It." Player 2 passes to 4, player 5 posts up strong side, and players 4 and 5 play the two-man game. If 5 is not open for the pass from 4, player 4 returns the pass to 2, player 5 "hooks" around 3's screen, and the early offense first swing options result.

    If 1 is in control on the left side, he passes to 3 to initiate the pattern and the players' roles are reversed.

SPECIAL TACTICS VERSUS STUNTING DEFENSES

In order to combat the adjustable stack attack, some opponents resort to "stunting" tactics.

Defeating the Front and Back
Double-Team Stunt

One stunt that you are certain to encounter is the "front and back double-team" on player 2. In executing this maneuver,

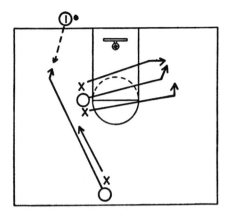

Diagram 2-22

the defender responsible for player 1 disregards him and doubles on 2. Defenders X1 and X2 "sandwich" 2 by playing him "front and back" prior to the inbounding of the ball. This tactic is an effective counter to 2's option of running straight at the ball, as described in Diagrams 2-20a and 2-20b.

To counter this stunt, adjust as follows: Player 2 clears to the weak side, taking the two double-teaming defenders with him. Player 3 charges into the area vacated by 2 and receives the inbounds pass from 1. If the defense is in a zone set, the area is completely open. If the defense employs a man-to-man defense, player 3's charge to the ball, augmented by a change of direction cut, frees him for the pass. (See Diagram 2-22.) After the inbounds pass is completed, the basic attack continues.

Countering the Run-Jump Stunt

Another frequently attempted surprise tactic is the run-and-jump maneuver in which a defender "off the ball" leaves his assigned man and runs at the dribbler in an attempt to surprise him. In Diagram 2-23, X2 forces 2 to dribble toward the middle. Defender X4 runs at 2 as X2 retreats down the line of the ball to obstruct the passing lane between players 2 and 4. The counter for this scare tactic must be timed perfectly. Player 2,

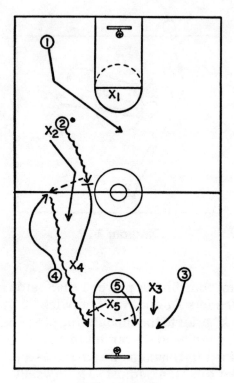

Diagram 2-23

reading the run-and-jump perfectly, slows his dribble, and passes to 4 at the precise moment that X2 begins his retreat. Player 4 *circles* to a position outside the line of the ball, receives 2's pass, and dribbles toward the basket, looking for a scoring opportunity.

This particular run-and-jump stunt can be attempted from various spots on the court, but our approach is always the same. The timing must be exact and every player must be ready to react spontaneously to this surprise defensive gamble.

COPING WITH DISGUISED DEFENSES

We occasionally meet an opponent who attempts to disrupt our press attacks by showing a zone set and changing to a man-to-man coverage (or vice versa) after we inbound the ball. Rather than play into their hands by changing our strategy in midstream, we disregard the spread adjustment and run our basic stack attack, adding simple adjustments when practical.

As stated earlier, the basic adjustable stack attack has proved to be effective in operating against any defense. The disguised defense is no exception.

METHODS OF TEACHING
THE ADJUSTABLE STACK ATTACK

During the preseason and periodically thereafter, you will find that a simple five-on-five drill is an efficient way to familiarize your players with the various passing routes and options. Assign each player the number of the position that he is to practice. (Some players, of course, will play more than one position and must be assigned to alternate accordingly.)

Have your players align in the designated spots (1-2-3-4-5) behind the endline. The coach or a manager will then score a lay-up and player 1 will enter the court and retrieve the ball as 2, 3, 4, and 5 sprint to their proper positions. (See Diagram 2-24.)

As player 1 steps inbounds to retrieve the ball, the coach calls a number combination that "names" the passing route and the subsequent option. For example, the coach calls "1-2-1-3-4 shoot!" This signals the play pattern to be run as follows: 1 moves out of bounds and passes to 2; 2 returns the ball to 1, who relays to 3 on the weak side; 3 passes to 4 for a baseline jumper. In teaching this pattern, advise player 3 that he may advance the ball on the dribble prior to hitting 4. (See Diagram 2-25.)

Another call might be as follows: "2-2-1 zone attack—1-5-4-break." This triggers the three-man break attack. (See Diagram 2-26.)

There are many combinations that may be called, and it is advisable to come to practice with a few combinations written in your practice plan so that you can fire them rapidly and sensibly. Be certain to remind the inbounder to vary the in-

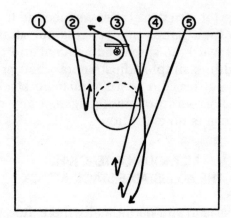

Diagram 2-24

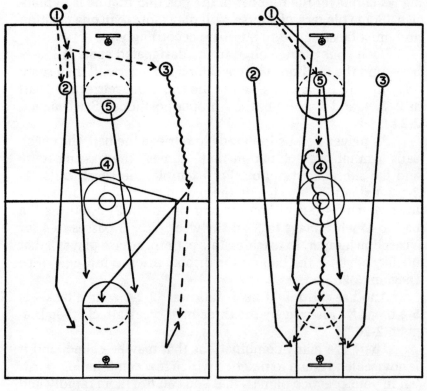

Diagram 2-25   **Diagram 2-26**

bounding side. Also check the position of player 4; remind him that he must sprint directly ahead of the ball when in the basic stack attack.

You naturally will wish to *simulate game conditions* by attacking the various defensive sets that are likely to be encountered in games. Scouting reports will be of value in planning for specific opponents. However, to be on the safe side, some practice time must be devoted to each type of press because you never know what the opponent may use against you. Work particularly against the 1-2-1-1, the 2-2-1, and the man-to-man presses as these are used most often.

In addition, be sure to work against those presses that allow the ball to be inbounded without pressure as well as those that exert extreme pressure on the receivers. Some presses trap the ball handler immediately while others wait until the dribble begins—don't fall into this trap, as it is exactly what the defense is waiting for! Be ready for anything and you will be worry free. So will your players!

POINTS OF EMPHASIS IN TEACHING THE ADJUSTABLE STACK ATTACK

When teaching the adjustable stack attack, the following principles must be firmly established:

1. Players 2, 3, 4, and 5 must align *quickly* as player 1 delays slightly before moving into inbounding position.
2. Read the defense quickly and react according to patterns of movement that have been established in practice sessions.
3. Look for the long pass to player 4 as a first option.
4. Teach your dribblers that they must never pick up the ball until a clear passing lane to a teammate is present.
5. Teach and stress the technique of "running through the ball."

6. Stress that each player is a potential pass receiver when the ball is controlled by another.

7. Work on player 1 "stepping in behind the ball." Use the backward relief pass often in drills and in game-type practice sessions.

8. Each receiver must turn and face the defenders to determine his next option.

9. Constantly remind the players that "The defense determines the play!" This applies both before and after the ball is inbounded.

10. Players "off the ball" must come to the ball when it is evident that the ball handler is *approaching* trouble. To wait until he is *in* trouble will be too late!

11. Work on passing to the receiver's "open side" (the side away from the defense).

12. Perfect the "one-hand catch" and the "under the chin—arms at right angle" ball protection technique.

13. Drill often on the three-man break attack. It is a primary scoring option versus zone pressure.

14. Use a stopwatch to time the quickness of preliminary aligning, putting the ball in play, and the ten-second time limit in the backcourt advance.

SUMMARY

The adjustable stack attack is an attack formation that ensures efficient inbounding of the basketball and provides sound attack principles for advancing the ball into the front court with precision and control. The objectives of the attack are twofold: (1) to score if the opportunity occurs as a result of our planned attack (no "freelancing"), and (2) to advance into the front court with the purpose of setting up a halfcourt pattern.

As the experienced coach will understand, it is virtually impossible to diagram and explain every possible situation that will occur in attacking backcourt pressure. Your philosophy as coach should be to teach your players to observe the basic rules and objectives of the adjustable stack attack. You should also encourage them to use their common sense if an unexpected situation arises during the the course of a practice session or a game. Impress on each player that "good things will happen" if he "protects the basketball, keeps his head up, and looks for a teammate!" This assurance works wonders in instilling confidence in players—and, of course, plenty of confidence is needed when attacking pressure!

We have found the adjustable stack attack to be entirely satisfactory in every respect. Our players over the years have been very comfortable with it, and the coaching staff is "sold" on it because it has consistently done the job on all levels of competition.

3

Defeating Zone, Man-to-Man, and "Stunting" Defenses with the Overload and Wing-Swing Patterns

EVOLUTION OF THE OVERLOAD
AND WING-SWING PATTERNS
AS MULTIPLE ATTACKS

The original overload and wing-swing pattern was designed to defeat the 2-1-2 and 2-3 zone defenses. However, as we continued to experiment, we incorporated additional movements and options that proved to be equally successful in combating odd-front zones as well as match-up zones and man-to-man defenses.

In addition, the use of one alignment to attack effectively any halfcourt defense has solved one of our most perplexing past problems—the employment of changing or alternating defenses by the opponent.

Prior to our discovery of the overload and wing, like many coaches we ran zone offenses against zone defenses and man-to-man offenses against man-to-man defenses. This practice worked very well until our opponents began to switch defenses: They "zoned" our man-to-man offenses and "manned" our zone offenses!

Equally troublesome was the now-popular defensive tactic of signaling frequent changes in an attempt to confuse the offensive team. Needless to say, these defensive stunts caused us many frustrating moments. Fortunately, the overload and wing-swing patterns have eliminated the problem of adapting to the defensive "switch." We now continue to employ the overload and wing continuities to attack any halfcourt defense. Equally important, since the overload and wing patterns are multiple designs—applicable to both man-to-man and zone defenses without adjustment or adaptation—they are among our favorite halfcourt attacks to be implemented in the Set It Phase of the early offense transition patterns.

Properly executed, the patterns invariably produce high-percentage shots and afford adequate rebounding and defensive balance.

BUILDING THE OVERLOAD AND WING-SWING PATTERNS

The overload and wing-swing patterns are developed in four successive stages: the *inside slide*, the *double rotation*, the *triple rotation*, and the *five-spot double wing overload*.

The Beginning Formation:
Player Positioning and Capabilities

The overload and wing is always initiated from a tight 2-1-2 set. Players 1 and 2 set up in the guard spots at the top of the key, players 3 and 5 align at the low-post positions with the inside foot on the lane block, and player 4 shapes up at the high post.

The guard spots, 1 and 2, are filled by players who can shoot the basketball from both the top of the key and from the medium-distance "wing" position. Each must be capable passers and possess the strength necessary to execute a two-handed overhead pass from "wing to wing." Ideally, these players should be "true guards," since they must be familiar with attacking possible backcourt pressure and halfcourt trapping defenses. Since they initially align at the guard positions but will play the wing positions after the overload is accomplished, we refer to them as "guard-wings."

Player 3 always slides to the baseline corner on the first swing of the basketball. He must be an accurate baseline shooter, since this skill is vital to the success of the attack. The one dribble jump shot from 10 to 12 feet is frequently open. Rebounding ability is mandatory because this position rebounds every shot. The ability to maneuver from both the high- and low-post positions is also desirable due to the fact that the triple rotation pattern requires player 3 to play each spot occasionally.

Players 4 and 5 are usually the big forward and the center. They rebound every shot. In addition, each player must be able to maneuver and score from both the high- and low-post spots when operating in the double rotation and the triple rotation patterns. If players 4 and 5 can score from the baseline, the attack will be even more potent since the triple rotation pattern "rotates" each player to the baseline spot as the ball swings. Player 4 aligns initially at the high post and 5 on the low post.

Coaching Point: Players 1 and 2 may set up at either guard spot. Similarly, 3 and 5 must vary their low-post alignments from time to time in an attempt to confuse the defense.

Initiating the Inside Slide
Overload and Wing-Swing Pattern

Diagram 3-1 illustrates the initial set, a tight 2-1-2 formation. We initiate each overload and wing pattern from this alignment.

If the defense also shows a 2-1-2 formation, their defense can be a standard 2-1-2 zone, a man-to-man defense or a match-up zone. On the other hand, should the defensive set be a 1-3-1 or a 1-2-2 alignment, either set may be a true zone or a springboard for implementing a match-up zone defense. Even though you may not be certain how the defense will react after you have made your initial entry from the set formation, you will be able to "read" its initial set and initiate the appropriate entry move.

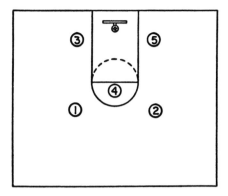

Diagram 3-1

The Short Wing Entry
Versus the Two-Man Front Defense

When the defense aligns in a two-man front, we immediately flow into our "short" wing adjustment (Diagram 3-2a).

In Diagram 3-2a, player 1 passes to 2 and cuts diagonally behind X2, stopping at the short wing spot. As 1 makes his cut, 4 slides strongside high to the "elbow"; 5 screens the baseline defender; and 3 uses 5's screen to form the baseline corner of the overload. Notice that after passing to 1, 2 moves to the wide wing position on the weak side. The basic "inside slide" has been accomplished, resulting in the overload and wing formation (see Diagram 3-2b).

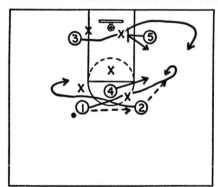
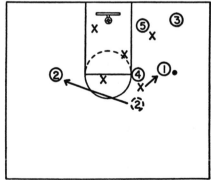

Diagram 3-2a   Diagram 3-2b

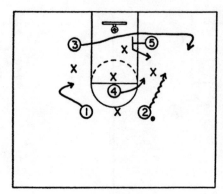 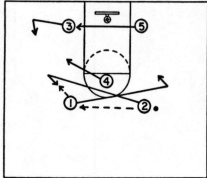

Diagram 3-2c　　　　　　　　　　Diagram 3-2d

The Dribble Wing Entry
Versus the One-Man Front Defenses

Since the 1-3-1 and the 1-2-2 zone defenses have a built-in coverage for our short wing entry scoring option (explained later in this chapter), we initiate the pattern with the "dribble" wing entry. As shown in Diagram 3-2c, player 2, reading the 1-3-1-defensive alignment, *dribbles* into the wing position as 3, 4, and 5 slide into the overload spots and 1 moves to the wide wing area on the weak side.

　　Coaching Point: The initial entry may be made to either side. However, you will notice that when the entry is made to the side of the court opposite player 3, the baseline screen by 5 is available. On the other hand, should the ball enter on the same side as 3, there is no screen since 3 always observes the rule of overloading the baseline to the same side as the first entry move. Also notice that 5 moves to the strongside low-post position to complete the overload (see Diagram 3-2d).

Teaching Relays, Counters, and
Change of Sides

After establishing the initial overload techniques and before exploring the scoring options, we teach five optional relay

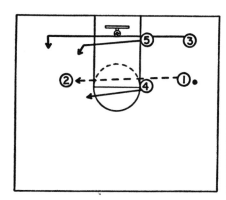 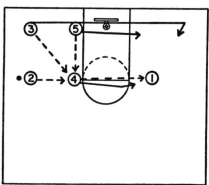

Diagram 3-3a   Diagram3-3b

methods and one countermaneuver, all of which result in a change of sides.

Wing-to-Wing Crosscourt Relay

The relay is merely a crisp pass from the short wing to the wide wing. As the ball is in motion, players 3, 4, and 5 move into the overload on the other side. This is called a "change of sides." (See Diagram 3-3a.)

High-Post Relay

This relay is a quick pass from the high-post player to the wide wing. (The pass to the high-post position may come from any strongside overload player.) In Diagram 3-3b, player 4 receives the pass from 2 or 3 or 5, and relays to 1 at the wide wing. Notice the change of sides as 5 moves to the low post, 3 runs to the baseline corner, and 4 slides to the strongside "elbow." Player 2 now becomes the wide wing.

High-Post Step-out Relay

When the passing lane to the high-post player is blocked by a defensive maneuver, the high post has the option of "stepping out" to receive the pass from the short wing (Diagram 3-3c).

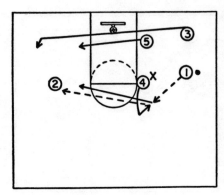 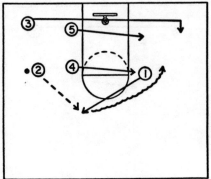

Diagram 3-3c   **Diagram 3-3d**

Point Dribble Relay

On occasion, the wide wing on the weak side will find it necessary to move to the point position in order to set up an effective relay. In this case, he takes the pass and dribbles into the short wing position as the inside players slide into the overload as usual (Diagram 3-3d).

High-Post Pick Relay

While this maneuver is basically a scoring option, it also presents an excellent opportunity for a relay to the wide wing and a change of sides. The high post sets a legal rear pick on the short wing's defender and executes a pick-and-roll play as the wing drives off the pick. The wide wing is frequently open as the defenders converge in an attempt to jam the pick-and-roll play (Diagram 3-3e).

Coaching Point: It is important that players 3 and 5 delay their change of sides until the wide wing receives the ball. To come too soon would nullify the open side pick-and-roll play. Also notice that the short wing assumes the wide wing spot after passing. Of course, if the pick-and-roll play produces a shot, the continuity terminates.

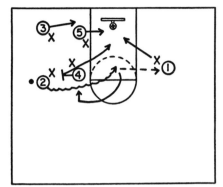

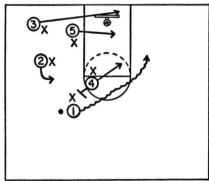

Diagram 3-3e   Diagram 3-3f

Countermaneuver

When a two-player front defense covers the short wing cutter with a man-to-man or with a front-line switch, allow the guard in control of the ball the option of countering either of these tactics by initiating a drive off the high-post screen. This move frequently results in a short jump shot by the driver. Notice that the change of sides begins as the guard begins his dribble. If no shot results, the overload has formed and play continues (Diagram 3-3f). (Also refer to Diagrams 3-5b, c, and d for additional discussion of countermaneuvers.)

Changing sides is vital to the success of the overload and wing-swing patterns. You will discover that the "accordion" action of the formation as it swings from side to side presents many inside openings. In addition, the quick relay options to the wide wing keep the weakside defender honest. If he sags deeply away from the wide wing to help defend the low-post player, the wide wing will be open for an unmolested 12- to 15-footer. On the other hand, should the wide wing be played tightly—or even halfway—the low-post defender must play behind or be subject to the open lob (Diagrams 3-4a and 4b).

Coaching Point: As the formation swings and the sides change, many scoring options will be readily apparent to the

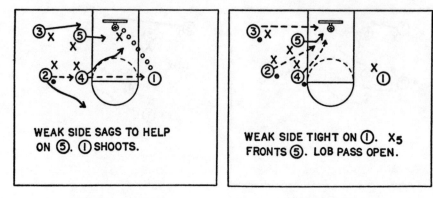

WEAK SIDE SAGS TO HELP
ON ⑤. ① SHOOTS.

WEAK SIDE TIGHT ON ①. X₅
FRONTS ⑤. LOB PASS OPEN.

Diagram 3-4a   Diagram 3-4b

players; however, if you allow scoring attempts before you thoroughly familiarize the players with the all-important relay methods, confusion will result.

Scoring Options of the Overload and Wing-Swing Patterns

The scoring options will be evident as the players practice the initial entries and the change-of-sides moves. Encourage any shot that is open and within the range and capabilities of the players. Emphasize certain fundamental options and plays. Your players will rarely have to change sides more than once to produce a good shot.

Short Wing Options and Counterplays

The key to the success of the short wing options versus the two-man front zones is the ability of the receiving guard (2 in Diagram 3-5a) to carry the "threat of the shot" in order to hold X2 on the ball to prevent the shot from the top of the key. As X2 defends 2, 1 cuts sharply to the short wing position, turns and faces the basket in a "shot-ready" stance and receives a short bounce pass from 2. At the same time, 3 sprints to the

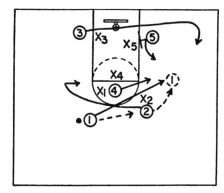 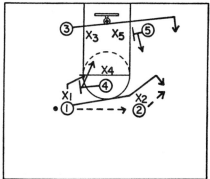

Diagram 3-5a   Diagram 3-5b

strongside baseline spot, using 5's screen on the backline defender, X5, and 4 moves to the strongside elbow. As illustrated
in Diagram 3-5a, the standard two-man front defense has a
difficult adjustment. Since X2 is defending 2, he cannot recover to 1 in time to prevent 1's shot. If X5 moves out to cover
1, both 3 and 5 (who rolls to the ball after screening) are open.
If X5 covers 3 and X4 drops to contain 5, both 1 and 4 are
open.

Another frequently used defensive tactic is to play the
short wing man-to-man as he cuts to the strong side. To counter
this stunt, we instruct 4 to set an inside screen on X1's high
side to prevent him from moving over the top of the screen.
In Diagram 3-5b, 1 passes to 2, drives X1 into 4's screen, and
runs to the short wing spot. As X1 tries to drop below the
screen in an attempt to stay with 1, 4 "rolls" one long step
toward the basket, completely defeating X1's defensive as-
signment.

Another countermove is equally effective. In Diagram 3-
5c, X1 is permitted to cover 1 man-to-man on the short wing
cut. Player 2, in possession of the ball, fakes the pass to 1, 4
screens X2, and 2 drives left off the screen for the jumper or
a pass to 3 or 5. Player 4 may also be open on a "mini" roll
toward the basket. Player 1 moves to the safety position.

This countermove also is effective to thwart the quick

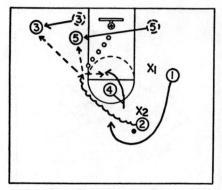 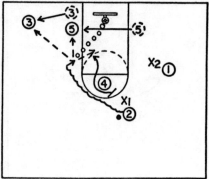

Diagram 3-5c   **Diagram 3-5d**

"switch" by X2 to cover the short wingman as X1 "switches" to contain 2 (Diagram 3-5d).

Coaching Point: Since the short wing entry is one of our most potent scoring options versus the two-man front zones, the basic play and the variations are stressed frequently in practice sessions.

Rebounding from the Overload and Wing-Swing Patterns

The rebound positions from the basic overload alignment must be emphasized—and reemphasized often. As shown in Diagram 3-6, 4 covers the weak side low; 5 fights for position in the middle of the lane; 3 moves strong side low to complete the rebounding triangle; 2 rebounds long at the foul line; and 1 is the safety man. A simple rule for the wings is as follows: The wide wing always rebounds long, and the short wing is always the safety man. *You will find that the most difficult problem is to get player 4 to rebound from high to low.* He must be drilled constantly on this all-important fundamental. (See Diagram 3-6.)

We continue to run the short wing options as long as the defense continues to play a straight two-man front zone. We also have had excellent success versus match-up zones that

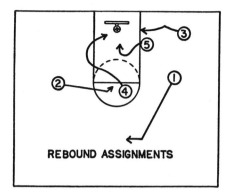

Diagram 3-6

use the 2-1-2 formation as a starting point. Of course, should the defense align in the 1-3-1 or the 1-2-2 formation, we implement the dribble wing entry as shown in Diagram 3-2c, or flow directly into the five-spot overload, which is explained later in this chapter.

 Coaching Point: You will notice that player 3 is always open for a shot along the baseline if 5's screen is effective. If 3's defender eludes the screen by 5 in order to cover 3, 5 is open on his step to the ball. Even though other initial entry options are often available, we have been so effective with our short wing game that we rarely need to explore them! Indeed, a change of sides is almost never necessary.

High-Post Turn Options

High-Post Turn Options have been extremely productive. The high-post player must maintain a position at the elbow no farther than one step below the foul line. (To move lower will obstruct the passing lane to 5 and make it possible to cover both 4 and 5 with one defender.)

 The high post receives the pass, turns away from the direction of the pass, faces the basket squarely, and looks for the shot. He may also fake a shot and execute a one-dribble jump shot; consequently, he must not dribble during his turn to the

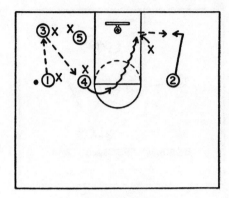

Diagram 3-7

basket. Always stress the high-post shot options during the first one or two times down the court. This is done in order to pull the middle defender "up" so that 4 can pass "down" to the low-post player for an easy shot. Of course, the high post may pass to 1, 3, or 5, each of whom maneuvers to free himself in his overload areas. (Remember that there is no change of sides until the ball is relayed to the wide wing!)

The high-post turn and drive move is particularly effective versus man-to-man defenses since the high post's "turn away from the direction of the pass" will place him in an excellent position to drive to the side away from the overload. The high post can also pass off to the wide wing in case the weakside defender switches to contain the drive (Diagram 3-7).

Coaching Point: In the basic overload and wing patterns, never make an initial entry from either guard spot to the high post. All high-post feeds will come from the players on the overloaded side after the overload has been formed. As pointed out later in this chapter, a direct initial entry pass to the high post from the guard spots triggers the "5-Spot" overload, which does not require a change of sides.

High-Post Reverse Option

The high-post reverse is an option afforded the high-post player when the low post is in control of the basketball. One

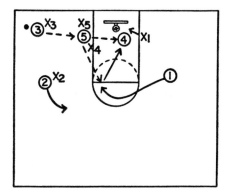

Diagram 3-8

defensive tactic that you are sure to encounter is that of the high-post defender sagging down to help out on the low-post player. A good way to keep the high-post defender honest is to reverse the offensive high post to the weak side of the basket for a possible pass and a lay-up. In this "quickie" play, you also bring the wide wing to the foul line as a scoring threat should his defender remain in his sagged position to help out on the high post as he reverses (Diagram 3-8).

Low-Post Fan-Out Options

The low-post player must be adept at passing the ball from his low-post position to an open teammate at any position on the floor. This all-important fundamental is called "fanning the ball." Many high-percentage scoring opportunities result from these fan-out passes. The receiver is encouraged to take the open, "in-range" shot immediately or maneuver for a one-dribble jump shot before passing off. Of course, you want the low-post player to maneuver for his shot whenever practical; however, you will find that the low-post opportunities are better and more often available after he has fanned-out a couple of times for scores by teammates!

As previously mentioned, the high-post pick option and the countermaneuver are also proven shot producers. As you will discover when drilling on the relay methods, the wide wing will be open time after time, providing that the relay is quick and crisp! *Without doubt, the unique placement of the wide wing is one of the innovations that have made the over-load and wing-swing patterns successful.*

THE DOUBLE ROTATION OVERLOAD AND WING-SWING PATTERN

Once the basic slide patterns and the relay and scoring options are mastered, it is a simple matter to implement a slight variation that we term the double rotation.

The double rotation is an interchange action between the high- and low-post players. The duties of the baseline player and the guard-wings remain as explained previously. The basic set, the initial entry moves, and the various relay options do not change; however, as the ball is relayed and the change of sides occurs, the low-post player breaks strongside high and the high-post slides strongside low. Diagram 3-9a shows the double rotation following a high-post relay. Of course, the double rotation is repeated with each change of sides (Diagram 3-9b).

This variation is effective in attacking man-to-man defenses and match-up zones. All scoring options remain the same.

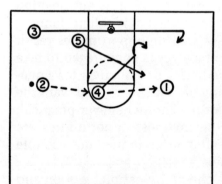

Diagram 3-9a

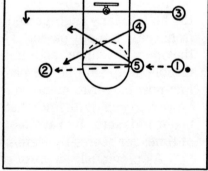

Diagram 3-9b

THE TRIPLE ROTATION OVERLOAD
AND WING-SWING PATTERN

In the triple rotation adjustment, players 3, 4, and 5 alternate playing the baseline, high-post, and low-post positions as the sides change. Again, the basic set, the initial entry moves, the relay options, and the scoring plays remain the same. The duties of the guard wings also continue as usual.

The initial entry options are explored and the basic slide overload is accomplished as shown in Diagram 3-2a, b, and c. On the first change of sides, the high-post player moves to the low post, the low post cuts to the baseline spot, and the baseline player sprints to the high-post position to complete the overload (Diagram 3-10).

If necessary, the triple rotation continues, as shown in Diagram 3-11.

The triple rotation pattern always follows the same routes: high to low; low to baseline; baseline to high. The triple rotation was invented to combat match-up zone defenses, and it has proved to be more than satisfactory in doing so. The triple rotation is a very good zone breaker and an excellent man-to-man offense. It is obvious that the pattern requires 3, 4, and 5 to possess the talents required to play three different positions. Not every team is so fortunate! However, as your

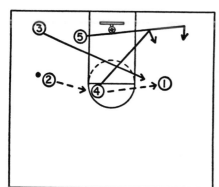

Diagram 3-10

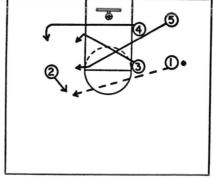

Diagram 3-11

basketball program develops, you will be able to develop mul-tiposition players by means of individual drills that stress the necessary skills.

Note: For those of you who compete under the restrictions of a "shot clock," let me assure you that we have conducted a number of controlled scrimmages and have played experi-mental contests using a 30-second shot clock. We have ex-perienced no problems. In addition, two acquaintances, both head coaches of Women's Division I collegiate teams, and whose teams compete under the restrictions of the 30-second clock, have enjoyed success with the overload and wing-swing pat-terns and report that the shot clock is "no problem."

THE 5-SPOT DOUBLE-WING OVERLOAD PATTERN

The 5-spot double-wing overload pattern differs from the over-load and wing patterns in that the 5-spot pattern attacks the defense from the *front* rather than from the *side*. Another vari-ation is that the "guard-wings" flare out and fill the wing spots, joining 3, 4, and 5 in a five-player overload (Diagram 3-12).

Of course, this 2-1-2 "5-spot" is nothing more than the

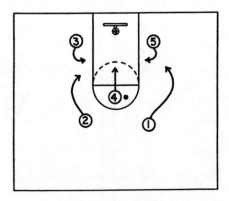

Diagram 3-12

old standard attack versus point zones. *However, it was not until we added the flaring guard options that we experienced greatly rewarding results!*

The 5-spot double-wing overload pattern is particularly effective in demolishing the 1-2-2 and the 1-3-1 zones. Since each player is an immediate scoring threat and is only one pass removed from the ball, the normal defensive coverages are disrupted. No continuity is necessary because a high-percentage shot is available almost immediately.

Attacking the 1-2-2 Zone Defense

The pattern is keyed by an initial entry pass from either guard to the high-post player. The high post, upon receiving the ball squares up to the basket, reads the defense and reacts accordingly. If the lane is open ahead of him, as in a 1-2-2 zone, he has the option of taking the shot or driving to the hoop to force a defensive switch by X3 or X5, which frees 3 or 5 for a pass and a short shot. Notice that guards 1 and 2 flare out slightly, fill the wing spots, and continue moving forward—*always maintaining a position within 4's peripheral vision* (Diagram 3-13).

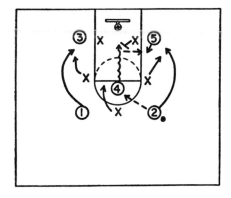

Diagram 3-13

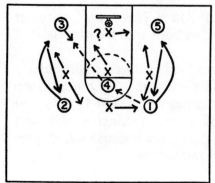
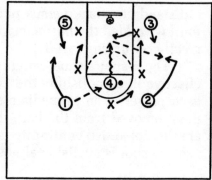

Diagram 3-14   Diagram 3-15

Attacking the 1-3-1 Zone Defense

The 1-3-1 zone also is vulnerable to this simple attack. Player 4 squares up as 3 and 5 "split" the baseline defender. If either is open, 4 makes the scoring pass. In the event that X4 retreats to help the baseline defender, 4 can shoot. Players 3, 4, and 5 rebound the "triangle" and 1 and 2 move back to the top of the key (Diagram 3-14).

Coaching Point: The practice of *flaring the wings* makes it impractical for the defensive wings to sag off and help defend the basket area. If they do so, 4 can make a scoring pass to the open wing. Diagram 3-15 shows this scoring option versus the 1-2-2 zone defense.)

The 5-spot, when used in conjunction with any other overload and wing-swing pattern, will afford complete satisfaction—no matter what defense you run up against.

SPECIAL DRILLS FOR PERFECTING
THE OVERLOAD AND WING-SWING PATTERNS

Since the scoring options of the patterns are basic fundamental basketball, few special teaching techniques are necessary.

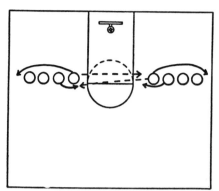 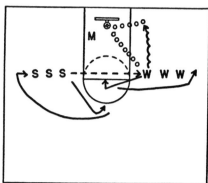

Diagram 3-16   Diagram 3-17

However, the relay options, the timing of the change of sides, and the defensive recognition and attack methods must be emphasized before the patterns are "game ready."

1. The Wing-to-Wing Crosscourt Relay Drill is a simple two-on-zero routine. All players, regardless of position, participate in this drill since the two-hand overhead pass is a fundamental that all players must master.

In the first phase of this drill, two guard-wing lines are established and the ball is "zipped" from wing to wing. After a player passes, he rotates to the end of his line and the drill continues (Diagram 3-16).

In the second phase of this drill, only the guard-wing players participate while the inside players move to other baskets and drill on individual shots and maneuvers from the high-post, low-post, and baseline positions.

We designate the lines as wide wing and short wing, with the wide wing being the shooting line. The short wing executes the overhead pass to the wide wing, who shoots the set shot or a jump shot off the drive. This drill also stresses our usual wing rebounding responsibilities. The wide wing, after shooting, rebounds the "long" area at the foul line and the short wing moves back to the safety spot. The short and wide wing sides are changed after each player has performed two complete rotations at each position (Diagram 3-17).

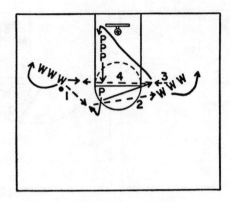

Diagram 3-18

Coaching Point: A manager or a designated player re-trieves the short rebounds and, should the wide wing rebound the shot at the foul line area, he is rewarded with a second shot.

2. The High-Post Relay and the High-Post Step-Out Relay are practiced in a three-on-zero drill. The guard-wings align at the wing spots; and the high-post, the low-post, and the baseline players alternate at the high-post relay position. On the first wing-post pass, the post steps out, receives the pass, relays the ball to the other wing, breaks strong side high, re-ceives a return pass, and executes the high-post relay. After the second relay pass, the post moves to the end of the "post line" and a new post steps up. Each wing makes one pass, then rotates (Diagram 3-18).

Note: The countermaneuver and the high-post pick play (Diagrams 3-3e and 3-3f) are taught as parts of our basic fun-damental offensive two-on-two drills. In addition, the short-wing options, the high-post options, the low-post fan-outs, as well as the individual player options which are integral parts of the overload and wing-swing patterns, are most efficiently learned via the five-on-zero and the five-on-five drills. No breakdown drills are necessary.

PERFECTING THE TIMING
OF THE OVERLOAD AND WING-SWING PATTERNS

The Five-on-Zero
and Five-on-Five Halfcourt
Progression Drills

Exact timing of player movement is essential during the initial entries as well as during the change of sides. The five-on-zero halfcourt progression drill is extemely helpful in perfecting the timing.

In implementing this method, we explain what we want; walk through it; point out important details and the "dos" and "don'ts"; then walk through it again. Be sure to explain and walk through the pattern from both sides of the court since the position of the baseline player determines the nature of the initial slide. (Refer to Diagrams 3-2a and 3-2d.)

Following a satisfactory "walk-through" session, progress to a "jog-through" and finalize with a "run-through" session. Repetition of the progressions will be necessary for only one or two practice sessions.

The next step is to repeat the progressions using five "token" defenders. During this phase, demonstrate the various techniques of the low-post, the short wing options, and so on. Explain the reasons for the various relay options. Remember that you are not ready to engage in actual scrimmage; scrimmaging should be permitted only after making certain that the players are comfortable with the initial entries, the slides, and a relay option or two.

Naturally, you will be able to accomplish a great deal of reteaching during scrimmage sessions, and, of course, the players will be eager to get into action after the "walk, jog, and run" progressions.

You will find that the progression method practically guarantees that your players will be going full tilt within four or five days.

TEACHING DEFENSIVE RECOGNITION AND ATTACK

Since the overload and wing-swing patterns have been devised to attack any defense, it is mandatory that your players learn to recognize the various defensive sets that they are likely to encounter in competition. For this reason, *each defense must be taught before your players can learn to recognize and attack it*—a seemingly insurmountable task, but a task that must be accomplished.

The logical starting point for this defensive teaching "program" is with your own team defenses. For example, if your regular halfcourt defenses include the man-to-man augmented by a 2-1-2 zone and a 1-3-1 zone, practice attacking these defenses before moving on to other defenses. The remaining basic zone defenses and combination defenses—the 2-3, the 1-2-2, the 1-3-1 "halfcourt trap," the box-and-one, the triangle-and-two—should then follow, one by one, in the teaching progression.

The final phase of the teaching program, recognizing the defensive change, has been practically accomplished since your players have already been thoroughly indoctrinated in "recognition and attack." All that remains is to "program" a defensive unit with some defensive change strategies, and to test the offensive attackers during a full-court scrimmage. For example; Huddle with the defensive unit and instruct them as follows; "Your basic defense is man-to-man. Change to a 1-2-2 zone after you score a field goal; 1-3-1 halfcourt trap after a made free throw. Play a 2-3 zone on all baseline out-of-bounds play, and stay in it until you gain control."

Continue to program defensive changes until all possibilities have been covered.

As the basketball season progresses, scouting reports will be of great help to you when preparing for specific opponents. However, these specific preparations will prove to be more successful and far less time-consuming because you and your players have been through it all before.

Coaching Point: Teaching all defenses is a time-consuming and tedious chore. On the other hand, you will discover that the many hours devoted to completing this essential teaching program have been well spent. *Not only have you improved your attack but also your team defenses!* Your players may become so proficient in simulating the other defenses that you will be able to incorporate one or more into your own defensive repertoire!

SUMMARY

Remember that each overload and wing-swing pattern is a separate unit of attack. Also remember that the five-spot double wing overload is *always* included as a complement to one of the others.

The provision for a change of sides in the event that the initial entry options do not produce a shot provides the offensive team with excellent inside openings as the defense shifts to cover the swing.

You will be pleased with the unique alignments of the wings and with the quick relay methods, screens, and counters that frequently lead to a score.

If the technique of "flaring" the guard-wings is new to you, this simple adaptation may be just the tactic you need to destroy the point zones.

All in all, the overload and wing-swing patterns include sensible basketball options, provide effective and easily learned continuities, and offer even the experienced coach some new ideas!

4

Attacking
Man-to-Man Defenses
with the Double-Screen
Multiple-Option Pattern

THE DOUBLE-SCREEN MULTIPLE-OPTION PATTERN

This is one of our favorite attacks versus the man-to-man defenses. First used as a single-option play to free a player for a shot behind a double screen, we continued to add other scoring options until the play evolved into its present form—a multiple-option continuity pattern.

THE INITIAL SET AND PLAYER REQUIREMENTS

The initial set is a tight 2-1-2 formation with players 3 and 5 positioned on the lane blocks, 4 at the high post and guards 1 and 2 aligned in offset positions at the top of the key.

Player 5 is required to set a good screen, shoot the short jumper from the bottom half of the foul circle, and rebound every shot.

Player 4 is primarily a screener and rebounder.

Players 1 and 2, in addition to possessing the usual play-making skills, must be proficient at performing the pick-and-roll and the give-and-go plays.

Player 3 is the key. The play is always initiated on his side of the court, and he may set left or right, with 5 filling

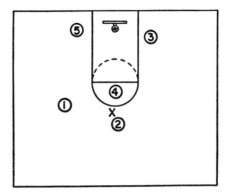

Diagram 4-1

the low spot on the opposite side. Player 3 also must be adept at executing the pick-and-roll and give-and-go plays. In addition, he must be able to score on the medium-range jump shot, drive when the opportunity is present, score on the crossover lay-up, and play both the low post and the wing spot in the two-man game.

In order to set up the defense for the initial pick-and-roll option, the guards must align in offset positions with the wide guard on the side opposite the starting position of player 3 and the middle guard at the exact top of the foul circle (Diagram 4-1).

Coaching Point: The offset guard alignment places the defender on the middle guard in an ideal position to be rubbed off on the initial pick-and-roll option.

Executing the Double-Screen Multiple-Option Continuities

Option 1:
The High-Post Double-Screen Pick-and-Roll

This option begins with a pass from either guard to the other, each "keying" a specific opening maneuver. This guard-guard passing routine is a necessary tactic since it enables player 3 to "time" his initial cut.

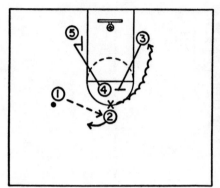

Diagram 4-2a   Diagram 4-2b

In Diagram 4-2a, player 1 is in control of the ball. As 1 passes to 2, 3 moves up and joins 4 to form a double screen at the high-post position. Player 2 fakes a drive toward the left side and drives to his right off the double screen.

Diagram 4-2b shows player 2 in control. Player 2 passes to 1 and screens X1 as 3 joins 4 to form the screen. As 1 drives off the "triple" screen, 4 clears away from the play and joins 5 to form a "shoulder-to-shoulder" double screen on the weak side. Both screeners face the strong side. The normal options of the pick-and-roll play are in effect: Player 1 can shoot the lay-up or the short jumper or feed 3 in the event of a defensive switch. Players 4 and 5 are in an ideal rebound position.

Option 2:
The Two-Man Game

The opening option usually produces a shot, but if both 2 and 3 are "covered," player 3 will post up and step to the ball in an attempt to set up a two-man game with player 2 (Diagram 4-3).

Coaching Point: Properly executed, the two-man game is one of the most productive options in any offensive attack that emphasizes low-post play! The rules are not complicated. The wing merely passes to the low post and executes a change-of-direction cut in order to free himself for a return pass. Since the wing is a scoring threat, his defender must continue to

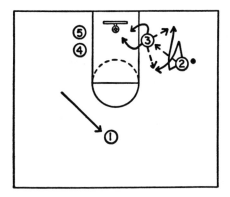

Diagram 4-3

guard him, thereby affording the low post the opportunity to maneuver for his shots. Our use of the two-man game has virtually eliminated the defensive tactic of "doubling down" on the post player. We practice the two-man game in a two-on-two drill that stresses the post-up fundamentals of "sealing" the defender, presenting a hand target to the open side, turn-around jump shots, short hook shots, and various power moves. The perimeter players practice the various passes, change-of-direction cuts, and shooting the quick set or jump shot upon receiving the return pass from the post player. Offensive rebounding is also stressed. We work on the two-man game during every practice session!

Option 3:
The Double Screen

After posting up with no results, player 3 remains at the low post as 2 relays to 1. Since 1 must move to the strong side to receive the relay pass, he must adjust his position by dribbling to the double-screen side before the double-screen option can be accomplished. As 1 begins his dribble, 3 crosses the lane, stops momentarily on the baseline end of the double screen and breaks to the ball when 1 is in position to make the pass. Notice that 2, after relaying to 1, replaces 3 at the low-post spot (Diagram 4-4).

If 3 is open and in range, 1 passes and 3 looks for the

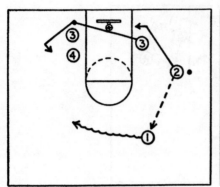 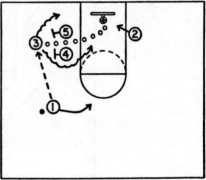

Diagram 4-4   **Diagram 4-5**

quick jumper. Player 3 may also execute a drive off the double screen if his defender eludes the screen in time to prevent the shot. The screeners move a step or two toward X3, setting a legal rear pick. Player 3 may drive either way (Diagram 4-5).

Countermaneuver

Should the passing lane from 1 to 3 be "clogged," or if 3 is in control and elects to pass back to 1, the counteroptions are implemented on the "cleared" side opposite the double screen.

Player 2, positioned on the lane block, has two choices;

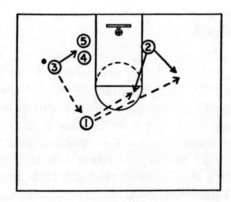

Diagram 4-6

He may cut to the wide wing position or break to the "elbow" on his side. The direction of his cut determines which counter-option will be run (Diagram 4-6).

The Wide-Wing Counteroptions

Option 1:
Reverse Action Ruboff

Player 2 cuts sharply to the wide wing, receives the pass from 1 and looks for 3, who attempts to free himself by rubbing his defender into the double screen. He always cuts over the top of the screen. If he is open, he receives the pass and moves in for a crossover lay-up shot. If he is not free to receive the pass, he stops at the low-post block (Diagram 4-7).

Option 2:
The Down-Pick

As 3 cuts over the top of the double screen, 4 headhunts X5, 5 breaks diagonally to the ball, receives the pass near the "dotted line," squares up, and shoots the jump shot. Players 3, 4, and 5 rebound the triangle, Player 2 rebounds long and 1 is the safety. Notice that after screening, 4 backs out of the lane to avoid the three-second violation and to free himself for a possible pass from 5 (Diagram 4-8). If 5 is unable to shoot, he looks for 2, 3, or 4 each of whom maneuvers to free himself

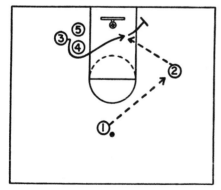

Diagram 4-7

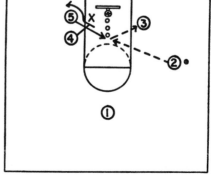

Diagram 4-8

for a scoring pass. If 5 does not receive the pass from 2, 5 and 4 exchange positions, and the offense is ready to begin again.

The "Elbow" Countermaneuvers

Should player 2 choose to break up to the "elbow," 3 moves out as safety and 1 and 2 play a two-man game on the cleared side.

Option 1:
The Give-and-Go Pick-and-Roll

Player 1 passes to 2 who keeps coming until he receives the ball. Player 1 runs a give-and-go cut down the cleared side of the court, 2 "floats" a pass to 1, pivots and rolls to the basket. The normal pick-and-roll options are explored. Player 1 is often open for a lay-up or a short jumper, and 2 is frequently open after a defensive switch (Diagram 4-9).

Option 2:
The Fake and Turn

Player 2 fakes the pass to 1, turns and faces the basket and shoots, drives or hits 1 with a late pass which is frequently open, as 1 flares out after his cut to the basket. Notice that 4 and 5 also flare away from the basket in a clearing action. They also may be open for a pass from 2 (Diagram 4-10).

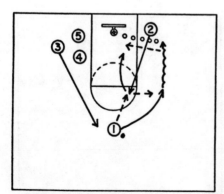

Diagram 4-9

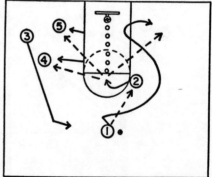

Diagram 4-10

Incorporating the Guard Clearout Entry

The last step in completing the double-screen multiple-option patterns is to incorporate an additional entry option. This option not only provides a different beginning look but also adds a simple but highly effective opening option, the guard clearout.

As usual, player 3 "keys" the entry option. He now breaks to the wide wing spot. Player 1 passes to 3 and clears away, joining 5 to form the weakside double screen. Player 4 moves to a medium-post position, halfway between the "elbow" and the basket, and steps toward the ball. Player 3 hits 4 and the two-man game is on. Player 4 may maneuver for his shot, or fan out to 3 who uses change-of-direction cuts to free himself. Of course, 3 may go one-on-one immediately or after receiving a fan-out pass. Players 4, 5 and 1 rebound the triangle, 3 rebounds long and 2 is the safety (Diagram 4-11).

Should 4 be unable to shoot or complete a pass to 3, he relays the ball to 2, the out guard. Similarly, if 3 is in control and cannot elude his defender or pass to 4, he passes to the out guard. In either case, this "relief" pass triggers the usual double-screen option as 4 moves around the screen, 2 dribbles over to make the feed, and 3 replaces 4 on the low-post block (Diagram 4-12). From this point on, all options unfold as described earlier.

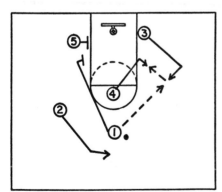

Diagram 4-11

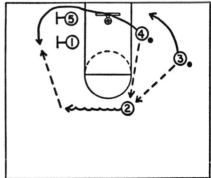

Diagram 4-12

Coaching Point: Of course, the guard clearout option requires that 4 learn to perform the options previously performed by 3. In addition, 3 must play the guard's roles in the countermaneuvers; the clearing guard becomes the top screener; and 5's duties remain the same. A minimum of reteaching is necessary.

Properly timed and executed, one of these options is certain to produce a desirable scoring opportunity. The standard rebound triangle, the long rebounder, and the safety position must be stressed after each shot.

SUMMARY

The double-screen multiple option pattern is an ideal man-to-man attack. The patterns include many of basketball's time-tested standards: The pick-and-roll, give-and-go, and the two-man game. Picks on and off the ball are effectively employed.

Teams of average size will find it to be an ideal three-guard offense with the third guard assuming 3's role.

Furthermore, the options are programmed in a smoothly flowing, highly effective continuity. The countermaneuvers consistently produce high-percentage shots. The "elbow" options quickly exploit the "open half" of the front court.

The timing of the various cuts are quickly learned via the Five-on-Zero and the Five-on-Five Progression Methods. The "elbow" options are integral parts of our regular fundamental practice drills. The all-important rebound patterns are consistent with those of our other pattern offenses. Consequently, a minimum of reemphasis is necessary.

The various options have been explained and diagramed as right-side attacks. If the majority of your players are right-handed—which is most often the case—the right-side attack is preferred. Should your players be ambidextrous, particularly players 1, 2, and 3, the attack will be doubly potent since you can initiate the offense to either side.

Perhaps the best selling point for the double-screen multiple-option patterns is the fact that the players love it! The various options include something for everyone. The 4 position is ideal for the kind of player that many coaches have: "Not much on offense, but a tough rebounder who can set a good screen and play some defense."

5

Beating Man-to-Man Defenses with the Cut, Shuffle, Pin-Down, and Drive Patterns

THE CUT, SHUFFLE, PIN-DOWN, AND DRIVE PATTERNS

These patterns are an effective blending of four time-tested attacks versus the man-to-man defenses. Each pattern in the continuity triggers a series of scoring options that produce favorable shot opportunities, good rebounding positioning, and safe defensive balance.

Equally important, each pattern is keyed by a distinctive player movement; therefore, a minimum of vocal and manual signaling is necessary. In addition, the continuities take full advantage of the desirable objective of "letting the defense name the play."

THE INITIAL ALIGNMENT

The beginning formation is illustrated in Diagram 5-1. The guards move into balanced positions approximately 12 feet apart. Two of the "down" men align in a double stack on one side, and the other sets up on the "single-side" low-post block on the opposite side.

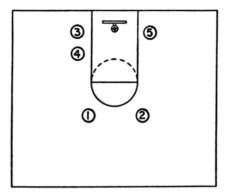

Diagram 5-1

Coaching Point: The initial alignment should not be stereotyped. The "down" men may stack right or left and may assume either the top or bottom position. The tactic of changing setup spots each time down the court should be emphasized since this variation creates different coverage problems for the individual defenders.

Initiating the Offense

The Pop-Out Techniques

The attack begins with a "pop-out" action by the "down" men. Their movement to the ball is predicated on the readiness of the guard to pass the ball inside. Instruct them not to "pop" until the ball-handling guard is in position to make the pass. If the timing is not right, an aggressive defense will force the receiver out of effective working position. In other words, you want the wings to receive the pass at the free throw line extended about ten feet from the sideline.

The pop-out technique allows the "down" men to break to different positions as the attack forms, thereby creating additional problems for the defenders.

The top player in the stack usually keys the pop-out positions. If the top man cuts to the high-post position, the bottom

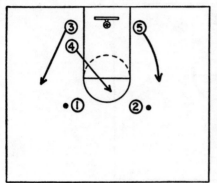 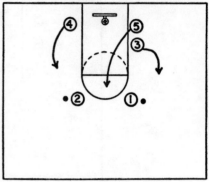

Diagram 5-2   **Diagram 5-3**

man breaks to the wing on his side as the "singleside" player moves to the wing on his side (Diagram 5-2).

Should the top man elect to break to the wing, the bottom man cuts to the high-post position, and so on (Diagram 5-3).

Designating a Key Cutter

On occasion, we designate a player other than the top stack man to function as the "key." He may align top or bottom on either side, another man fills the other stack spot, and the third sets on the "single side." The key man is always the first cutter and may "pop" to the high post or to the wing. The second stack man moves to the vacant spot (Diagrams 5-4a and 5-4b).

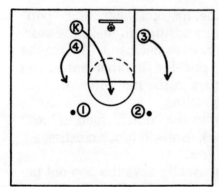 

Diagram 5-4a   **Diagram 5-4b**

DEVELOPING THE ENTRIES, THE SCORING OPTIONS, AND THE CONTINUITIES

Either guard may initiate the pattern by performing one of six possible entry maneuvers, each of which keys specific options. (We encourage an occasional pass from one guard to the other prior to implementing an entry move.)

> *Entry Maneuver 1*
> *Guard Passes to Wing and Executes a Basket Cut*

In Diagram 5-5, guard 1 passes to 3, makes a change of direction cut to the basket and looks for a scoring pass. Player 3 must pass to the cutter as soon as he "opens."

The shuffle cut is the second option in this continuity. As 1 cuts to the basket, guard 2 aligns his position in a straight line with the high post and the basket. He delays two counts and "shuffles" to either side of the high post. Notice that 1, the first cutter, has not freed himself for a pass from 3 and has moved to a strongside baseline position. If 2 is open, 3 passes to him for a shot. The high post is the safety man and the others rebound. This is the standard rebounding pattern following all shot attempts (Diagram 5-6).

Coaching Point: When we first introduced the cut and shuffle options, we cleared the first cutter to the weak side in an attempt to open the area for the shuffle cutter. However,

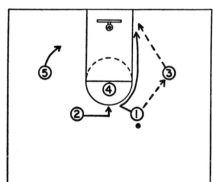

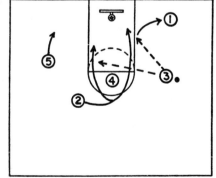

Diagram 5-5   **Diagram 5-6**

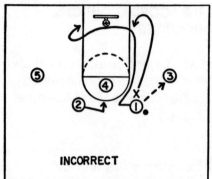

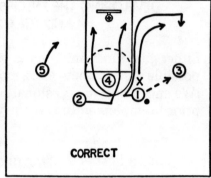

Diagram 5-7   Diagram 5-8

we found that the defender on the first cutter frequently allowed the cutter to clear, only to remain on the strong side in
a "ball-you-man" position to defend the shuffle cutter's move
to the basket. Diagram 5-7 illustrates the incorrect route for
the first cutter.

To counter this defensive stunt, we rerouted the first cutter to a strongside position. This tactical change established
the first cutter as a *continuous scoring threat*, forcing his defender to stay with him all the way. This adjustment also
improved the scoring potential of the Shuffle Cut Option because it eliminated the extra defender and doubled the effectiveness of the option since the cutter could now break to the
basket on either side of the high post. Diagram 5-8 illustrates
the correct procedure.

The *pin-down options* are a natural continuation of the
cut and shuffle options. In Diagram 5-9, as the shuffle cutter
moves past the high post, 4 fakes a roll to the basket, hops
back toward the ball, receives a pass from 3, and faces the
basket. Simultaneously, the wings, 3 and 5, move to the baseline and "pin down" the defenders on 1 and 2.

Coaching Point: The fake roll—actually a long step toward
the baseline as the second cutter moves past him—is vital to
the success of the Pin-Down options. The high post must force
his defender to loosen up sufficiently to enable him to receive

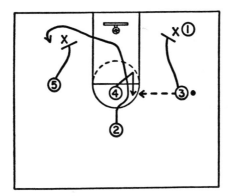

Diagram 5-9

the ball within the outer half of the foul circle. This maneuver must be emphatically stressed! If the high post is forced to take the pass outside of the circle, the options are not as effective because the post player will be out of the high-percentage shooting area. This will allow his defender to drop back and help defend the pin-down plays.

As the wings complete their pin-downs, the baseliners break sharply off the screens and the options unfold:

1. The high post may maneuver for his shot.

2. The high post may pass to either cutter, who may maneuver for a shot or play the two-man game with the screener who posts low (Diagram 5-10).

3. The high post may feed the screeners who roll parallel to the baseline, take the pass, and shoot the power lay-up (Diagram 5-11).

4. If the screeners have not opened by the time they reach the foul lane on their side of the court, they come up the lane and "beg" for the ball. If either receives the pass, he can turn and shoot, work with the wing on his side, look for possible backdoor plays, pass to the opposite side screener, and so on. The formation now resembles a 1-4 alignment (Diagram 5-12).

5. The pin-down options usually produce a great shot.

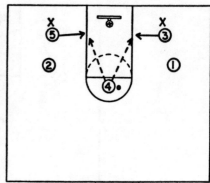

Diagram 5-10   Diagram 5-11

However, in the unlikely event that the high-post player is unable to find an opening, he passes to either wing and the two-man game resumes.

6. Whenever the wing returns the ball to the high-post position, both wings pin down again, and the options are repeated. Diagram 5-13 shows player 1 in control. He passes to 4 and pins down on X3 as 2 screens for 5. The roles of the four perimeter players are now reversed, creating an additional problem for each individual defender. The repick option is very productive.

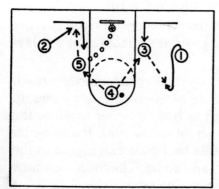

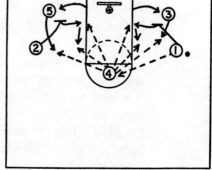

Diagram 5-12   Diagram 5-13

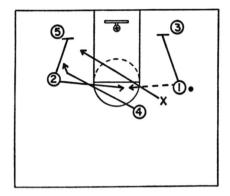

Diagram 5-14

You may run it two or three times, working for a super shot.

Coaching Point: Notice that the high-post player has remained in his original spot throughout the entire continuity. While it's better that he does so, defensive pressure which forces him to receive the pass outside the foul circle necessitates a countermaneuver: The high post interchanges with the weakside wing, who replaces him at the post. This action not only opens the passing lane, but also creates a "new" high post and a "new" wing. After the interchange, the patterns continue as usual (Diagram 5-14).

"Popping" Versus Halfcourt Pressure

Defensive pressure—or lack of it—determines the distances that the players must travel on the initial "popout." If the defense is sagging, the guards advance to the top of the circle and the "down" men break to the ideal position—foul line extended, ten feet in from the sideline.

On the other hand, if the defense is pressuring at or near halfcourt, the offense must initiate higher. Regardless of the setup positions, the options and continuities are always the same as previously explained. Diagram 5-15 illustrates the initial entry possibilities against halfcourt pressure. We welcome

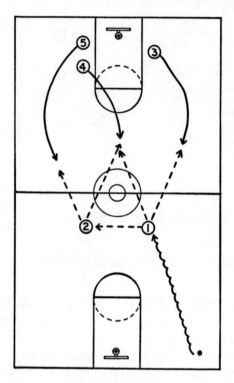

Diagram 5-15

any form of halfcourt press since this pressure affords the cutter a greater distance in which to "outrace" his defender to the basket, resulting in easy lay-ups.

Coaching Point: In explaining the movement "up the lane" by the screeners in Diagram 5-12, the term *"beg"* is used, since the word accurately describes what the players in this situation need to accomplish. Stress to your players the fundamentals of moving to the ball with arms extended at right angles to the floor in a "begging" position. Frequently remind these cutters that if they really want the ball, they must "beg" for it. Constantly remind the high post to "hit the beggar!"

Entry Maneuver 2:
Guard Direct Dribble Toward the Strongside Wing

If the wing defender attempts to deny the guard-to-wing pass, initiate the offense with a dribble entry.

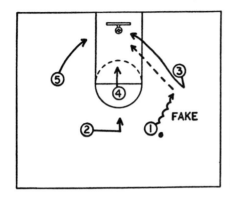
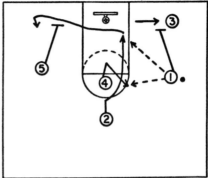

Diagram 5-16a   Diagram 5-16b

The "Backdoor" Option

In Diagram 5-16a, guard 1 dribbles toward wing 3, executes a convincing fake pass to him, and 3 takes one long step toward the ball with the left leg, "begging" for the ball. He then brings the left leg back through in a crossover step and explodes to the basket in a backdoor cut. If open, he has the lay-up; if not, 3 moves to the strongside baseline (since he is in reality the first cutter), 1 assumes the strongside wing and looks for 2 on the shuffle cut as shown in Diagram 5-16b. If 2 is not open, the pin-down options follow.

> *Entry Maneuver 3:*
> *Guard Pass to Wing and Cut Outside of Receiver*

Another method of starting the offense is the outside cut by the passing guard. This entry affords the offense a different look and adds two optional scoring maneuvers, the *delayed shuffle cut* and the *wing drive*.

The Delayed Shuffle Cut Options

Guard 1 passes to 3, cuts to the outside of the wing and receives a return pass. The high post reads the key and moves to the weakside baseline spot as 3 breaks to the vacated high-post position, sets a screen and 2 shuffles to the hoop. If no score results, 2 moves into pin-down formation (Diagram 5-17).

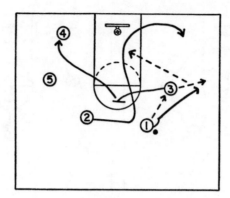

Diagram 5-17

Coaching Point: Notice that 3 now operates at the high post. Another result of this initial entry maneuver is that both guards are on the same side, allowing them to play together in the pin-down options—a definite plus for two fundamentally sound guards!

The Wing Drive Options

A second optional scoring maneuver from the outside cut entry is the wing drive.

Since you don't want the wing to stand and wait while the shuffle cut option develops, instruct the wing to execute a good foot fake toward the baseline. This fake causes the wing's defender to retreat slightly, thereby creating a more favorable passing lane to the shuffle cutter. On the other hand, if the defender does not react properly, the wing drives past him and goes for the lay-up or the short jumper. If the wing drives, the shuffle cutter discontinues his cut and replaces the driver at the wing position (Diagram 5-18a).

Forming the Pin-Down Alignment

If the driver cannot obtain a good shot, he dribbles to the baseline area, stops, pivots, and passes back to the "new" wing, who relays to the high post. The pin-down plays continue (Diagram 5-18b).

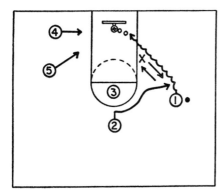

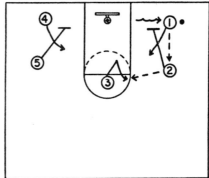

Diagram 5-18a   **Diagram 5-18b**

Entry Maneuver 4:
Guard Pass to Wing and Screen for Weakside Guard

The guard-guard screen also provides a powerful entry variation, the *high double-screen series.*

Guard 2 advances on the dribble, passes to 4 at the wing, and sets an inside screen on X1. Guard 1 cuts off the double-pick set by 2 and 5, takes the pass from 4, and shoots the lay-up or the short jump shot (Diagram 5-19a).

As 1 cuts to the basket, 2 steps back and "slashes" past the high-post screen, executing the shuffle cut. Again, if no shot is available, the pin-down formation results (Diagram 5-19b).

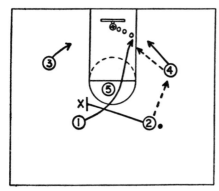

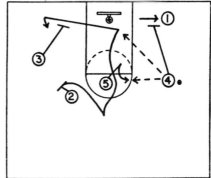

Diagram 5-19a   **Diagram 5-19b**

Entry Maneuver 5:
Guard Pass Directly to the High Post

The guard-to-high-post initiation presents additional coverage difficulties for the defense. Since the majority of the beginning keys involve a guard and a wing, a quick pass to the high post provides an effective variation to the attack.

Wings' "Backdoor" Option

Guard 1 hits the high post as he "pops." Players 3 and 4, who have "popped" to the wings, reverse to the basket. Player 5, maintaining his back-to-the-basket position, looks for the quick backdoor pass to an open wing (Diagram 5-20a).

The High-Post–Guard Split Option

Notice that the guards in Diagram 5-20a have veered slightly toward the sidelines after passing to the post. This is a necessary maneuver for two reasons: (1) to afford the high post and the wings a few seconds to complete the backdoor play; (2) to set up X1 and X2 for the secondary option, the *high-post split.*

In Diagram 5-20b, since guard 1 is the passer, he cuts first and 2 is the second cutter. If either cutter is *ahead of his*

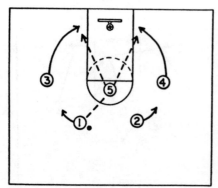

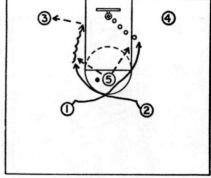

Diagram 5-20a   **Diagram 5-20b**

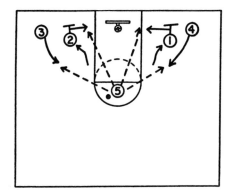

Diagram 5-20c

defender, 5 passes and the receiver "plays it by ear"—shooting, driving, passing, and so on.

Forming the Pin-Down Alignment

If the "split" does not produce, the guards continue their cuts, pin down on X3 and X4, and the usual options ensue (Diagram 5-20c).

> *Entry Maneuver 6:*
> *Guard Drive Between High Post and Wing*

In addition to the cut, shuffle, and pin-down continuities, the drive play has proved to be an effective play option, not only as an initial quick action shot producer but also as a complement to the aforementioned patterns. The *drive play* is the basketball version of football's quarterback option play.

The Guard Drive Play

Diagram 5-21 illustrates the drive play as an initial option. Guard 1 advances and the down men "pop" as usual. However, 1 now continues his dribble and penetrates toward the basket between the high post and the wing. Of course, the options are obvious: The "quarterback" may drive to the "goal" or "option off" to the rolling high post or to the flaring wing as dictated by the defensive coverage. The drive play is a "ter-

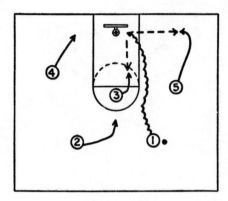

Diagram 5-21

minal" option; that is, if no shot results, the formation resets and play begins with the usual "pop outs." Players 1, 3, 4, and 5 rebound; 2 is safety.

Coaching Point: It is important that the high post remains *slightly behind the line of the ball* as it advances in order to make room for the driver to go all the way. In addition, this trailing position will afford the high post an open short jump shot if his defender switches to cover the dribbler.

The Shuffle Play Countermaneuver—The "Burn" Play

In addition to using the drive play as an initial entry option, we also employ it as a counter option to the shuffle play. This highly effective use of the drive play has been termed "the burn." In other words, we use the drive play to "burn" a smart defender who attempts to "play the play"!

For example, assume that the continuity is progressing in the usual manner: Guard 1 has passed to wing 3 and has made his basket cut. The second cutter prepares to shuffle, but he observes his defender sagging behind the high post, awaiting the shuffle cut—a common defensive tactic. If the shuffle cutter moves to the basket, the "waiting" defender will be able to deny the pass to the cutter by employing "ball-you-man" coverage (Diagram 5-22).

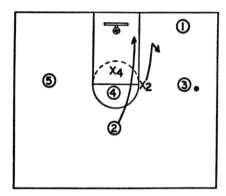 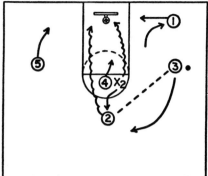

Diagram 5-22   **Diagram 5-23**

If you do not counter this defensive stunt, the effectiveness of the shuffle cut as a potent scoring option will be severely minimized, if not eliminated completely. Fortunately,
the drive play "burn" option not only counters this defensive
stunt but actually improves the effectiveness of the shuffle cut
as a scoring weapon.

The drive play "burn" option is detailed in Diagram 5-
23. Wing 3 has the ball, and 2, setting up for the straight cut
shuffle, notices that his defender is "waiting" below the high-
post position. Guard 2 "baits" the defender by holding his
position, taking a pass from 3, and "setting" for the outside
shot from the top of the circle. Defender X2 has two alterna-
tives: He can hold his retreated position and "gamble" on a
missed shot, or he can choose to move out and contest it. If
X2 elects to defend against the outside shot, 2 waits until he
assumes a guarding position directly in line with the high post
and the basket, then he "burns" the defender by driving him
into the high-post screen. Of course, 2 may drive to either side.
This excellent countermove usually results in a lay-up by the
driver or in a pass to the high post as he trails the play. Both
of these options are solid shot producers. Naturally, the baseline man on the strong side and the wing on the weak side are
also scoring threats in the event of a defensive switch (Diagram
5-23).

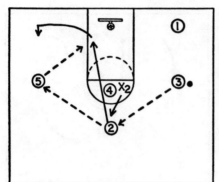 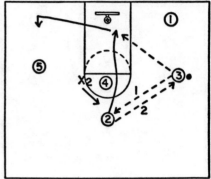

Diagram 5-24a   **Diagram 5-24b**

The Delayed Shuffle "Burn" Play

A second method of "burning" a retreated shuffle cut defender is the "delayed shuffle." We like this option because it naturally results in the familiar pin-down formation.

The delayed shuffle "burn" play is set up in the same manner as the drive play. With X2 retreated and waiting, 2 holds, receives the pass from 3, and carries the threat of the outside shot. If X2 moves out to cover, 2 passes to the side *opposite the direction of the defender's cut*, and explodes to the basket—leaving X2 "hanging" on the high-post screen. The usual pin-down positioning is implemented if the delayed shuffle fails to score (Diagrams 5-24a and 5-24b).

Coaching Point: The *Guard-Guard Screen Option* (Diagrams 5-19a and b) is ideal for setting up the drive and the delayed shuffle burn plays. The guard screener has the option of stepping back and holding for the return pass or shuffling immediately. If he holds, he may execute either burn play.

PERFECTING THE OPTIONS AND CONTINUITIES OF THE CUT, SHUFFLE, PIN-DOWN, AND DRIVE PATTERNS

As you study this chapter, you will undoubtedly arrive at the accurate conclusion that sound individual fundamentals and precise execution are vital to the success of these power-packed patterns.

In addition to the standard passing, dribbling, shooting, and rebounding drills, adequate practice time must be devoted to teaching the techniques of cutting, shuffling, pinning down, begging, backdooring, driving, and burning.

The following breakdown drills greatly enhance the learning process:

1. *The Initial Cut Drill* (Diagram 5-25). Player 2 "pops" to the wing spot, receives pass from 1, executes change of direction cut, cuts to the basket, receives the pass from 2 and shoots a lay-up or a jump shot. Player 2 may pass to the cutter at any point during the cut. Players 1 and 2 rebound and rotate after the shot. Two balls are used. Sides change at the direction of the coach. One or more baskets may be utilized.

2. *The Shuffle Drill* (Diagram 5-26). (Football blocking dummy is used to simulate the high-post screener.) The drill begins with 2 in possession of the ball. Player 1 aligns in *straight line*, rubs off to either side of the high post, takes pass at any point on his route to the basket, and shoots the lay-up or the jumper. Players 1 and 2 rebound and rotate. Two balls are used.

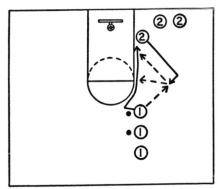

Diagram 5-25

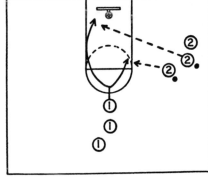

Diagram 5-26

3. *The Pin-Down Drill* (Diagram 5-27a). The drill begins with the ball at wing. Player 3 fakes a roll to the basket, hops to the ball, and receives the pass from 2. Player 2 pins down on imaginary X1 and the pin-down options are implemented: Player 3 may shoot, feed 1 coming off the screen, or hit 2 on parallel cut. Players 1 and 2 rebound. Players rotate clockwise on right side; counterclockwise on left. Two balls are used. Change sides on command of coach.

   Coaching Point: Stress the screener's position: The screen must be stationary, slightly toward the basket side of the defender, and must be set as close as possible without making contact with the defender. In addition, the screener must maintain his set position until his teammate moves past him; then he pivots on his baseline foot, rolls to the basket parallel to the baseline, and looks for a pass from the high post.

4. *The Pin-Down and Beg Drill* (Diagram 5-27b). An extension of the drill in Diagram 5-27a. Screener 2 cuts parallel to the baseline, then comes up the lane, "begs" for a pass from 3, receives the pass and either shoots the jump shot or feeds 1 on the "backdoor" cut. Two balls. Rotate as explained for Diagram 5-27a.

5. *The Initial Entry Drive Play Drill* (Diagram 5-28a). Player 1 drives the slot, shoots or options to 2 or to 3 who

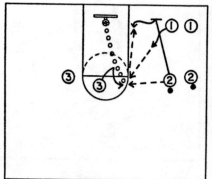

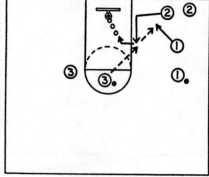

Diagram 5-27a   Diagram 5-27b

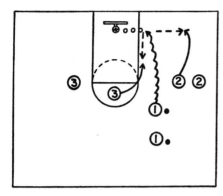 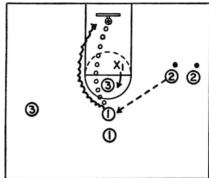

Diagram 5-28a   **Diagram 5-28b**

trail. Players 1, 2, and 3 rebound. Rotate and repeat. Use two balls. Change sides following three or four repetitions.

6. *The Drive Play Burn Drill* (Diagram 5-28b). Ball in control of 2 who passes to 1. Player X1 defends 1 and varies his defensive side and his "stunts." If X1 sags and waits, 1 shoots and 2 and 3 rebound; if he moves out to defend, 1 drives in the opposite direction and 1, 2, and 3 rebound. Change X1 periodically. Three-man rotation. Use two balls. Change sides at the direction of the coach.

7. *The Shuffle Burn Play Drill* (Diagram 5-29). Same setup

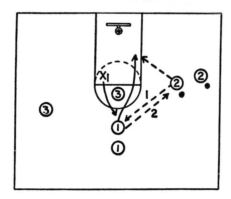

Diagram 5-29

as Diagram 5-28b. Player 2 passes to 1, 1 returns pass to 2 and counters X1's defensive "stunt" as usual. Players 1 and 2 rebound; 3 is safety man. Two balls are used. Three-man rotation. Change sides.

8. *The Five-Player Progression Drills* After the "breakdown" drills are satisfactorily established, the five-on-zero halfcourt progression drill will enable you to sharpen the timing of each segment of the offense. In addition, the alternate methods of initiating the patterns should be introduced. Of course, the five-on-five progression drill will follow; a "live" defense will further enable you to stress the fine points of execution as well as prepare the players for game situations. (See Chapter 3 for an explanation of progression methods.)

SUMMARY

The cut, shuffle, pin-down, and drive patterns are sound, sensible, and successful. Properly timed and executed, the play options together with the perfectly meshed continuities will handle any man-to-man defense! The varied "pop-out" techniques, the diverse initial entry options, and the various player position interchanges cause many problems for individual and team defenders alike.

Any one of the cut, shuffle, pin-down, and drive patterns may be employed as a single unit. You may discover that adding one or more of these plays to your own favorite offense will round out your total attack. Many coaches have done so with excellent results.

The drive and shuffle burn plays are *impossible* to defense. *If there is a "perfect" play in the game of basketball— the burn play is it!*

Even though you will not be able to teach and perfect the entire cut, shuffle, pin-down and drive offense in a few practice sessions, you will find that a little bit at a time works wonders! A slow but sure approach—though time-consuming and at times tedious—will reap future rewards that will delight even the most discerning coach!

6

Combating the
Zone and Combination
Defenses with the Pick, Beg,
and Flash Stack Attacks

THE PICK, BEG, AND FLASH STACK ATTACKS

These attacks are zone breakers *par excellénce!* Originally designed as a counterattack to the box-and-one and the triangle-
and-two combination defenses, the stack attacks also produce
excellent results against the conventional zones.

The patterns may be initiated from either a single or double stack formation, depending upon the individual skills of
the available personnel. The best selling point for both the
single and double stack formations is that both can be installed
in a few practice sessions. The scoring options are easily mastered and the continuity quickly learned!

FORMING THE DOUBLE STACK ATTACK

The *double stack attack* is ideal for two strong post players,
two accurate medium-distance shooters, and a capable point
guard. The post players will be required to "pick," "beg," and
"flash"; play the two-man game; and rebound aggressively. The
two best shooters will operate along the entire baseline area
and from the weakside wing positions. The point guard ini-

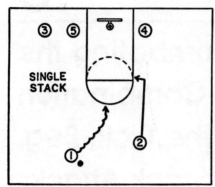

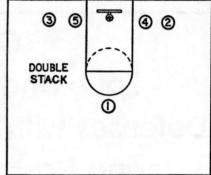

Diagram 6-1a   Diagram 6-1b

tiates the pattern and will also assume a weakside wing spot as the continuity develops.

The initial formations are shown in Diagrams 6-1a and 6-1b. Player 1 is the point guard; players 4 and 5 are the posts; players 2 and 3 are the baseline players.

Notice that the "stacks" are horizontal alignments instead of the usual vertical stacks along the foul lane. The posts align on the low-post blocks; the baseliners shape up approximately three feet from the post; all players face the basket.

INITIATING THE DOUBLE STACK ATTACK

Declaring a Side

The point guard initiates the pattern by dribbling toward the top of the key before "declaring a side." This declaration of side is merely a protected dribble to either the right or left side and keys the players' movements.

For example, if player 1 in Diagrams 6-2a, 6-2b, and 6-2c declares "left," 5 screens the bottom defender on his side and 3 "pops" back, *parallel to the baseline*; 4 screens for 2 (if defender is present); and 2 "pops" to the weakside wing position at the "elbow." After screening for 3, 5 moves up the

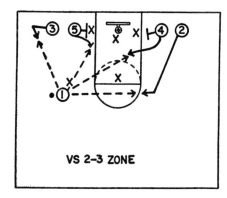

VS 2-3 ZONE

Diagram 6-2a

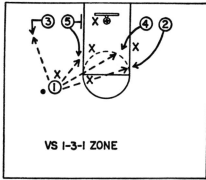

VS I-3-I ZONE

Diagram 6-2b

lane and 4 flashes a step or two into the lane, both "begging" for the ball. Player 1 now has four possible passing options. (If 4 is not open immediately on his "mini-flash," he backs out of the lane to avoid a three-second violation and assumes his original position.)

Of course, if player 1 declares to the right side, the players' roles are reversed.

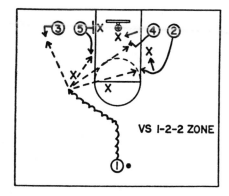

VS I-2-2 ZONE

Diagram 6-2c

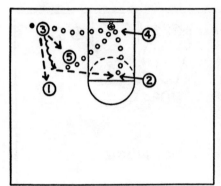 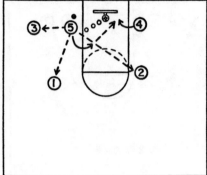

Diagram 6-3   Diagram 6-4

SCORING OPTIONS

If 3 receives 1's pass, he may shoot, maneuver for the jumper, play the two-man game with 5, pass to 2 "mini-flashing" from the "elbow" position, or return the ball to 1 (Diagram 6-3).

If player 5 receives from 1 or 3, he turns and shoots or "dumps" the ball to 4 for a power lay-up. He also may fan a pass to 1, 2, or 3 (Diagram 6-4).

CHANGING THE SIDES

The change of sides occurs whenever the ball is passed to the weakside wing. This pass may originate with any player; however, it usually occurs after an unsuccessful drive toward the middle by the baseliner, or as the result of a relay pass back to the point. Of course, the point may hit the weakside wing immediately; this also triggers the change of sides (Diagram 6-5).

As the ball is in motion toward the weakside wing, 3 cuts to the ballside baseline spot, using both 5 and 4 as screens. Player 5 "flashes" toward the ball immediately after 3 moves past, 4 "begs" after screening, and 1 moves to the weakside wing. Player 2 may shoot, pass to 3, 4, or 5, or return the ball to 1 at the elbow (Diagram 6-6).

Any further change of sides is accomplished in the same manner. Emphasize the baseline players rule to your team:

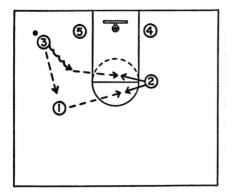

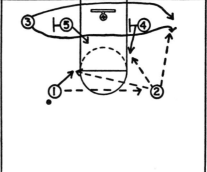

Diagram 6-5   Diagram 6-6

"Once a cutter, always a cutter!" Diagram 6-7 shows the change of sides after 2 returns the ball to 1.

Coaching Points:

1. The baseliner may cut either in front of the screeners or to the baseline side. In addition, the cutter may elude a defender by executing a zig-zag maneuver whenever practical (Diagrams 6-8a and 6-8b).

2. Both the strongside and the weakside posts must screen for the cutter prior to "flashing" or "begging." The weakside post (player 4 in Diagram 6-6 and player 5 in Diagram 6-7) is in excellent position to "headhunt"

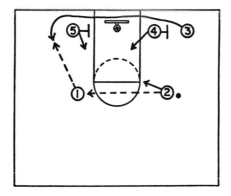

Diagram 6-7

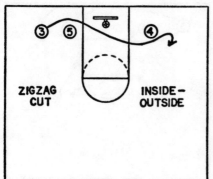

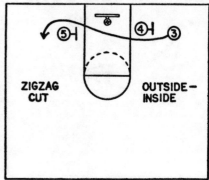

Diagram 6-8a   Diagram 6-8b

the defender who is in the best position to cover the cutter. These screening techniques are vitally important to the success of the baseline continuity.

3. While the diagrams and explanations have exclusively emphasized player 3 as the baseliner, if the point player's "dribble declaration" had been to the *right side*, player 2 would become the baseliner with 3 assuming the weakside elbow position.

INSTALLING THE SINGLE STACK ATTACK

If you have only one capable baseline player available, *the attack is initiated from a single-stack formation*, as illustrated in Diagram 6-1b. The pattern begins with either guard in control, the baseliner joins either post to form the single stack, and the guard initiates the pattern with a declaration dribble or by passing to the other guard who declares the side.

If the declaration is toward the stack side, the "off" guard immediately moves to the weakside elbow, and the usual "cuts," "picks," and "flashes" result (Diagram 6-9a).

On the other hand, *if the initial declaration is to the side opposite the stack*, the baseliner immediately cuts to the strong side, using the post screens. Again, the "off" guard fills the

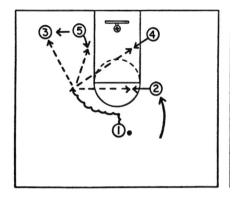 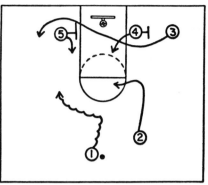

Diagram 6-9a   Diagram 6-9b

weakside wing position. This is the only change from the double-stack procedure (Diagram 6-9b).

UTILIZING THE PARALLEL CUT
TO EXPLOIT THE CONVENTIONAL ZONES

The parallel cut by the baseline player is an important change from the usual "pop out" toward the wing position, as explained in Chapter 5, "Beating Man-to-Man Defenses with the Cut, Shuffle, Pin-Down, and Drive Patterns." Since the two-player front zones are designed to cover the first perimeter pass by sliding a front defender to the ball, the deep position of the baseliner increases the distance between the baseliner and the front defender that effective coverage is difficult if not impossible. Naturally, the post screen must be effective and the baseline player must get the shot away quickly (Diagram 6-10).

Of course, the initial position of the back line defender determines the success of this quick shot option. If the back defender aligns between the baseliner and the post, the parallel cut is accomplished as usual, the back defender moves out with the cutter, and the post is usually open as he "begs" for the ball (Diagram 6-11).

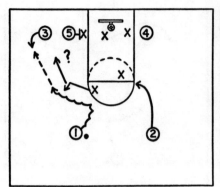
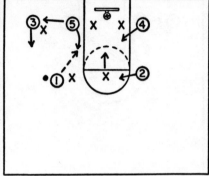

Diagram 6-10   Diagram 6-11

ATTACKING ONE-PLAYER FRONT ZONE DEFENSES

Scoring Options Versus the 1-2-2 Zone

The one-player front zones present even less of a challenge for the offense. The back defenders in the 1-2-2 zone must initially align close to the lane, making the post screen practically a certainty. Again, if the back defender eludes the screen, the screener is open coming to the ball. In addition, mini-flashes by the weakside post and the weakside wing create open passing opportunities (Diagram 6-12).

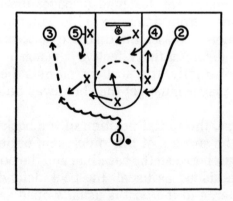

Diagram 6-12

Scoring Options Versus the 1-3-1 Zone

The standard 1-3-1 zone and the 1-3-1 halfcourt trapping zone are the most vulnerable of all, since the initial positioning of the single baseline defender makes him "ripe for picking"! In Diagram 6-13 player 1 declares right and continues his dribble until the defensive wing picks him up. Player 4 screens, and 2 takes the pass from 1 for the open shot.

Any attempt to trap either the point or the baseliner usually results in an easy lay-up or short jump shot since the "double-up" always leaves one player free. (We spend a significant amount of practice time on finding the open man versus the trapping defenses.)

Scoring on the Change of Sides

In the unlikely event that the first entry options do not succeed, the change of sides invariably results in a great shot. In Diagram 6-14, player 1 chooses to relay to 3. As the defense reacts to the change of sides, 4 picks X4, 5 also sets himself to pick X4 (or X5 depending upon the defensive coverage plan), and 2 sprints to the opposite side for the pass and the shot.

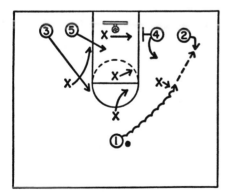

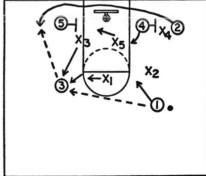

Diagram 6-13 · · · · · · · · · · · · · Diagram 6-14

DEFEATING THE BOX-AND-ONE
AND THE TRIANGLE-AND-TWO COMBINATION DEFENSES

Attacking the Box-and-One Defense

Both the box-and-one and the triangle-and-two combination defenses are attacked from the double-stack formation. Diagram 6-15 shows the box-and-one coverage versus the double stack: Player 3 is the "star" and is being defensed man-to-man.(Solid squares in the following diagrams represent man-to-man defenders.)

The continuity is the same as usual. As illustrated in Diagram 6-16a, if 1 declares right, 4 screens for 2, 2 receives 1's pass and shoots or passes to 4 if necessary. If 2 is a capable shooter, you can run this time after time and disregard 3 entirely. However the majority of coaches will scrap the defense in a hurry.

Baseline Player's Options

If 3 is the only baseline scorer available, 1 declares to his side. This brings 2 to the weakside wing spot and 3 becomes the sole baseline runner. Since X3 (designated by the solid square in the diagrams) is nose-to-nose with 3, 1 immediately changes

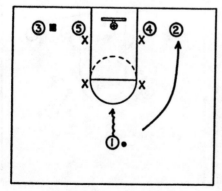

Diagram 6-15

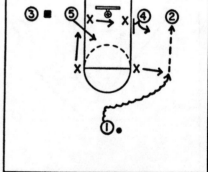

Diagram 6-16a

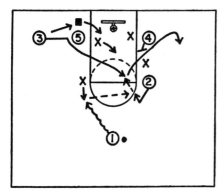

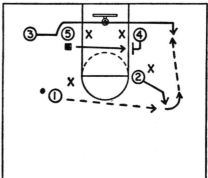

Diagram 6-16b   Diagram 6-16c

the side by passing to 2 at the weakside wing position. Player 3 now cuts directly at 5's stationary screen, notes the route of the defender, and reacts accordingly. (See Diagrams 6-16b, 6-16c, and 6-16d.)

1. Since X3 retreats to the baseline side of the screen, 3 pops into the lane for a pass from 2 and a quick turn-around jumper. If 3 is not open in the lane, he continues the cut off 4's screen (Diagram 6-16b).

2. If X3 fights over the top of 5's screen, 3 cuts to the ball side, again using 4's screen (Diagram 6-16c).

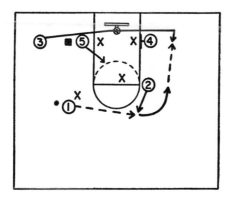

Diagram 6-16d

3. If the defender is "hung up" on 5's screen, 3 continues to the ball side where 4 head hunts the most likely defender (Diagram 6-16d).

Coaching Point: While it is good strategy to set up your best shooter as often as possible, *the other scoring options must not be overlooked.* If the defense gambles on stopping your star performer with a combination defense, it stands to reason that the defense will be less efficient at various other points. Exploit the "pick," "beg," and "flash" options of the stack attacks that are designed to take advantage of these open opportunities.

BEATING THE TRIANGLE-AND-TWO

The double stack pattern versus the triangle-and-two is an exact replica of the box-and-one attack. The normal continuity of the "pick," "beg," and "flash" attack forces the triangle-and-two to convert to a box-and-one! Consequently, you have the luxury of attacking either defense with the same offense. Diagram 6-17 shows players 2 and 3 being played man-to-man and the remaining three players aligned in a triangle zone defense. Player 1 declares right or left as usual. (He is often open for an unmolested shot if X1 "lays off.") Notice that when

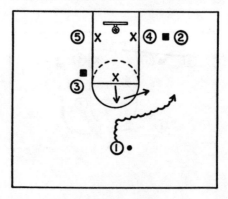

Diagram 6-17

1 declares toward 2, 3 moves to the weakside wing spot, X3 continues to cover him; therefore, 2 becomes the baseline runner and the continuity proceeds in the normal manner. Also notice that since X3 has been anchored at the wing, the defense has converted to a box-and-one. Since X3 is covering 3 closely, he must fake a basket cut and step back to the ball in order to free himself for a relay pass from 1.

Coaching Points: The stack attack explanations and diagrams assume that the baseline player or players are the objects of man-to-man coverage. If any other combination of defensive coverages is attempted, such tactics will prove to be equally ineffective. For example, if the point player is the object of man-to-man attention in a box-and-one defense, the baseline coverage is impossible as indicated in Diagram 6-18.

If both posts are defended man-to-man, the triangle-and-two cannot cover the baseline players without isolating the posts one-on-one. In addition, the change of sides would require the point player in the defensive triangle to cover both 1 and 2, or 1 and 3—a difficult task (Diagram 6-19).

A few moments of checking other defensive combination possibilities on the blackboard will assure you that the double stack pattern will successfully handle any zone coverage, conventional or otherwise.

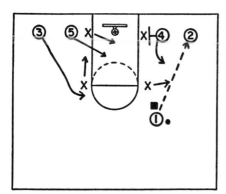

Diagram 6-18

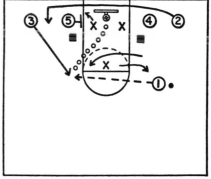

Diagram 6-19

TEACHING THE PICK, BEG, AND FLASH ATTACKS

As stated at the outset of this chapter, the pick, beg, and flash attacks can be installed with a minimum of teaching. As is true of the other power pattern attacks, properly designed and effectively taught fundamental drills will provide the necessary expertise.

Of course, the initial entries, the change of sides, the baseliner's cutting routes, and the flash techniques must be perfected. The employment of the now familiar progression methods will provide mastery in a short period of time.

SUMMARY

The pick, beg, and flash attacks are effective zone breakers.

The horizontal stack alignment has proved to be an effective baseline "shot-getter." The multiple baseline screens and the flashing techniques by the weakside wing and the weakside post produce many high-percentage shots. The rebound positioning is always assured. The innovative employment of the double stack attack as a counter to both the box-and-one and the triangle-and-two is not only an effective scoring machine but also a great time saver.

Most important, it does the job for which it was intended—it defeats the zone defenses!

7

Developing the Tandem Post Power-Pattern Variations

The tandem post offense is one of the old standards used to attack the two-player front zone defenses. An interesting description of the original tandem post attack appears in a 1962 edition of *Basketball Methods* by Pete Newell and John Benington:

> This offense may also be referred to as a "high-low" post setup. One inside man is placed at the foul line area and the other operates along the baseline. They may exchange positions from time to time to keep the defense from ganging up. The two wing men operate from the side of the court about even with the foul line extended and the outside man plays in the middle of the court. This offense resembles a normal 1-3-1 alignment used against many zone defenses. It may be classified as a personnel offense because the men do not move too much out of their positions. The man at the high-post area may move from one side of the foul circle to the other to receive a pass and may also screen for the middle man to drive to the basket. The baseline man usually moves with the ball; normally this is the position with good scoring opportunities in the tandem offense. Jack Nagle, former Marquette University coach, made good use of the tandem post offense in 1954–55 and his team did much to popularize it.
> The baseline man often stays on the opposite side of the court from the ball to allow the wing man the opportunity to drive

to the baseline or allow room for the middle man to drive to the basket using a screen set by the high-post man.

The middle man initiates practically every move. He can determine from which side of the court he wishes to start a play. He may pass directly to either of the inside men. He may also make use of a screen set by the wing men and drive to the outside for a shot. The wing men should be good outside shooters and capable of driving in for the jump shot."[1]

The above summation of the old tandem post is accurate in every detail. Many present-day coaches are employing the tandem post exactly as described—and with excellent results.

However, in order to cope with today's multiple defenses, we have augmented the old tandem post by incorporating new techniques. Our players now exchange and/or rotate positions; screening options have been added, and continuities have been developed. These variations have vastly improved an already great attack!

THE TANDEM POST POWER-PATTERN VARIATIONS

The Outside Interchange Maneuver

In order to keep the point defender from dropping down to help cover the high-post player and to prevent the weakside wing from sagging to the rear of the low-post man, we added the *outside interchange maneuver*. Player 1 passes to 3 and interchanges positions with 2, the weakside offensive wing. Defenders X1 and X2 move with 1 and 2, nullifying the "sagging" tactics of X1 and X2 (Diagram 7-1).

This variation practically ensures that our low-post player will be one-on-one since the weakside help has been eliminated. In addition, it makes impractical the fronting of the low post because to do so would invite the unobstructed lob pass from 3. If players 1, 2, and 3 can function at the wing positions

[1]Pete Newell and John Benington, *Basketball Methods* (New York: The Ronald Press Company, 1962)

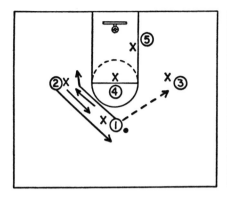

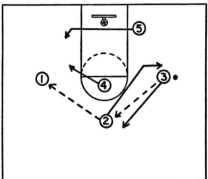

| Diagram 7-1 | Diagram 7-2 |

as well as at the point, the interchange can be accomplished with no loss in efficiency.

One possible disadvantage of the interchange maneuver is that it may rotate a key rebounder into the safety position at the point and a small guard into a primary wing rebounding spot. However, we believe that the advantages gained outweigh this possible disadvantage.

The outside interchange is effected each time the ball is relayed from the point to the wing. (Diagram 7-2).

The Wing-Under Variation

Another method of clearing the area for the low-post player is the wing-under maneuver. As player 1 passes to 3, weakside wing 2 sprints under the back line of the defense, uses 5 as a screen and sets up in the strong side corner (Diagram 7-3).

This maneuver makes 2 an immediate scoring threat and X2 must stay with him on the cut. Again, 5 is one-on-one with no weakside sag to hamper his maneuvering. Notice that 1, after passing to 3, moves toward the "wide" wing spot in an attempt to deter X1 from dropping to help on 4. Players 2, 3, 4, and 5 explore the strongside overload options explained in Chapter 3.

If no shot results, 2 replaces 3, 3 takes the point, and 1

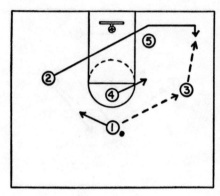
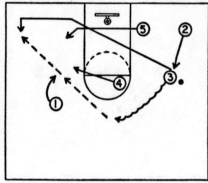

Diagram 7-3   Diagram 7-4

assumes the wing position and the attack continues. Should 3 swing the ball to 1, 4 and 5 slide across the lane and 2 runs under again (Diagram 7-4).

If 3 passes to 2, 4 and 5 hold their positions and 1 runs the "wing-under" (Diagram 7-5).

Coaching Point: The "wing-under" is equally effective against any zone defense or match-up zone since the defensive player charged with weakside basket coverage does not normally move all the way with the wing as he cuts under the defense. Diagram 7-6 shows the normal 2-1-2 zone coverage and the result:

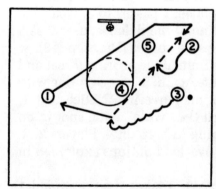
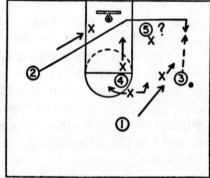

Diagram 7-5   Diagram 7-6

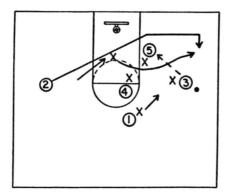

Diagram 7-7

Of course, should the weakside defender elect to continue to cover the cutter in a match-up adjustment, a man-to-man coverage would result and 5 would again have the advantage of a one-on-one position (Diagram 7-7).

The Wing-Baseline Exchange Variation

Since many of the skills required of the baseline and wing players are similar, exchanging their positions has proved to be a simple and effective addition to the tandem post offense. This exchange not only creates new problems for the man-to-man defenders but also for the zone coverages.

The exchange may be executed on either side of the court and is adaptable to both right- and left-handed personnel. Two methods of exchanging positions, the "pass and pick," and the "dribble pick," are utilized. In the pass-and-pick option, the wing passes to the baseline player, moves to an inside screening position and the pick-and-roll play results. Notice that in Diagram 7-8 player 4 stays high and 3 looks for an open gap on the weak side. Player 5 may shoot the jump shot, hit 2 rolling to the hoop, or pass to 4, 3, or 1.

Should no shot be available, 5 assumes the wing spot vacated by 2, 2 becomes the baseliner and the offense continues (Diagram 7-9).

The "dribble pick" maneuver produces the same options.

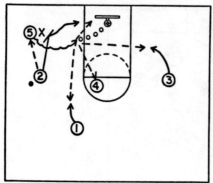

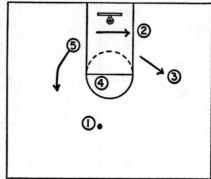

Diagram 7-8   Diagram 7-9

The only difference is in the initiating of the exchange: The wing dribbles to the baseline defender, stops, screens, passes to the baseline man and the pick-and-roll play results (Diagram 7-10).

The Low-Post Up-Pick Series

The low-post up-pick series is another of our favorite "quickie" attacks versus any defensive set.

The attack begins with a pass from the point to either wing. The series is keyed by the low post, who immediately

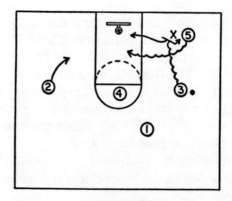

Diagram 7-10

moves up and sets a screen on the wing defender. The screen must be set slightly toward the baseline side of the defender, since the continuity of the series demands that the wing drive toward the baseline rather than toward the middle of the court.

The Up-Pick and Roll Play

The up-pick and roll play is illustrated in Diagram 7-11. Player 1 passes to 3, and 5 moves up and screens X3. Player 3 drives toward the baseline, 5 rolls to the basket, and 4 replaces 3 at the wing spot. Player 3 may shoot or feed 5 on the roll-in.

If neither 3 nor 5 is open, 3 pivots, passes to 4 at the wing, 5 posts low and a sideline triangle is formed. Player 4 is frequently open for a wing shot upon receiving a pass from 3, particularly if X4 has sagged into the lane area to help defend the pick and roll by 3 and 5 (Diagram 7-12).

The Sideline Triangle Options

If the up-pick and roll play fails to produce a good shot, a number of triangle options are available.

The Sideline Triangle Split Play

If the wing is unable to free himself for the good shot or feed the low post on the roll-in, he may dribble toward the baseline corner as the post-screener assumes the medium-post

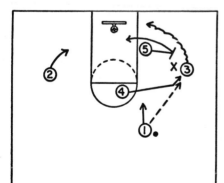

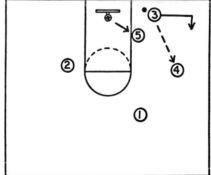

| Diagram 7-11 | Diagram 7-12 |

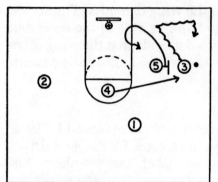

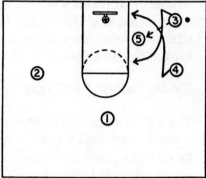

Diagram 7-13a   **Diagram 7-13b**

position, and the high post fills the vacated wing spot (Diagram 7-13a).

Player 3, the corner man, may pass to 5 at the medium post and run a split with 4. *The passer is always the first cutter and cuts to the side of the other perimeter player* (Diagram 7-13b).

If 3 cannot pass to 5, he passes to 4; 4 hits 5 and initiates the split (Diagram 7-13c). Player 5 has the option of passing to the open cutter or maneuvering for his shot.

Coaching Point: The sideline triangle "split" play versus the man-to-man defense is most effecive when the "splitters"

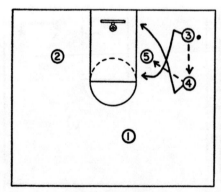

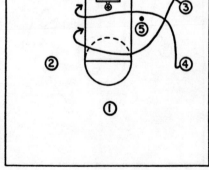

Diagram 7-13c   **Diagram 7-13d**

continue to move past the post, taking their defenders with them, and terminate at the weakside rebounding positions if neither receives a return pass. Of course, the post player has the option of the immediate shot and is not required to wait for the cutters to complete the split (Diagram 7-13d).

The Sideline Triangle Cut-and-Drift Maneuver Versus the Zones

The most effective triangle option versus the zone defenses is the "cut-and-drift" maneuver. Either the wing or the baseliner passes to the post. The baseliner always cuts to the basket parallel to the baseline in a "backdoor" attempt. If the baseline cutter is open, he has a lay-up; if not, he continues to the weak side as a rebounder. As the baseline man cuts, the wing drifts to the baseline area where he is usually open for a fan-out and a quick jumper. Diagram 7-14 illustrates the "cut and drift" maneuver and the usual zone coverage. Notice that X3 has two choices: He can cover 3's cut or pick up 4 on the "drift." In either case, he loses!

In addition to the triangle options, which are keyed by the high post's move to the wing spot as the pick and roll is executed, the high post may exercise a second choice: the post exchange option.

As the low post and the wing are maneuvering, the high-

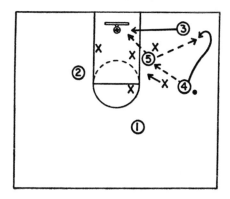

Diagram 7-14

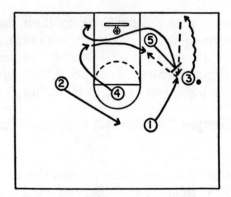

Diagram 7-15

post man cuts to the weakside block, player 1 replaces 3, and 2 comes to the point. If 3 cannot make a play, he passes out to 1. Player 5, seeing 1 at the wing spot, turns and heads for the weak side and 4 cuts off the moving screen and looks for the pass from 1 and an open lay-up or a short jumper. If no shot, the triangle options are again explored by 3 in the corner, 1 at the wing, with 4 shaping up at the medium post position (Diagram 7-15).

Coaching Point: Diagram 7-15 illustrates player 4 cutting off a moving screen. Of course, a "moving" screen is illegal. However, if 5 always cuts low and 4 comes high, a foul rarely, if ever, occurs.

When the ball is returned to the point position, each player either assumes the position that he "occupies" (Diagram 7-16) or resets in his original starting position, (Diagram 7-17). Of course, this is a coaching decision and will depend on the adaptability of your personnel.

Coaching Point: While the triangle options have been explained as a part of the low-post up-pick series, they can and should be used any time that the triangle formation occurs, no matter what variation is in effect.

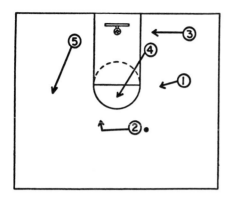

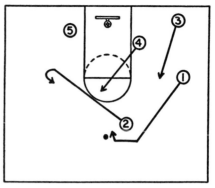

Diagram 7-16   **Diagram 7-17**

The High-Post Reverse Variation

Since the high-post reverse option proved to be such an effective shot producer in the overload and wing-swing pattern
(Chapter 3), we incorporated the maneuver into the tandem
post game. This variation not only produced backdoor lay-ups
for the high post, but also provided excellent low-post "fan-
outs" to the other players.

This play offers the high post the option of reversing to
the basket when the low post is in control. The pass to the
low post may come from the point, the wing, or the high post
(Diagram 7-18).

Diagram 7-19 shows the low post with the ball. Player 4
reverses to the basket, wing 3 maneuvers to free himself, 2
replaces 4 at the high post, and 1 gaps between the high-post
and wing spots. Every player is now a scoring threat since 5
can pass to any spot. The play can be initiated to either side
with 2 and 3 reversing their roles.

The High-Post Stepout Variation

We also "borrowed" the high-post stepout variation from the
overload and wing-swing pattern.

On occasion, the point player is forced to move to the

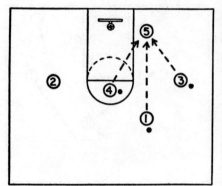 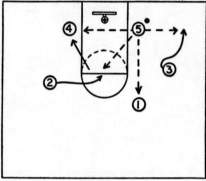

Diagram 7-18   **Diagram 7-19**

strong side in order to receive the outlet pass from the wing, particularly if the wing is stuck near the baseline. When this situation is present, the point maneuvers, receives the pass out, and the high post steps out to the top of the key. Diagram 7-20 illustrates the relay and the change of sides.

The Weakside Wing "Flash" Variation

At times, the defender on the point guard will attempt to steal the pass out from the wing. In order to counter this tactic, we program the weakside wing to "flash" into the high-post area and look for a pass from the strongside wing. Upon receiving

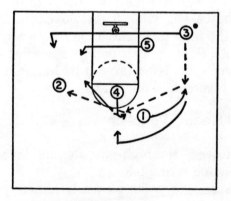

Diagram 7-20

the pass, he squares up and shoots or drives down the cleared side for a lay-up or a short jumper.

In Diagram 7-21, the triangle has formed and 3 has the ball. Player X1 is in a denial position on 1. The weakside wing 2 flashes, receives a pass, and maneuvers for a shot. Players 2, 4, and 5 rebound the triangle, 3 rebounds long, and 1 is the safety.

Coaching Point: The weakside flash play is effectively taught in two-on-zero and two-on-two drills. The drills emphasize "squaring up" and shooting as well as stressing the various driving maneuvers: the jab step, the crossover, the rocker step, etc.

The Double Screen Variation

The double screen play explained in Chapter 4 is also adaptable to the tandem post offense. Diagram 7-22 shows one method of implementing the double screen from the tandem post formation. Player 1 passes to 2, 4 clears weakside low, 3 joins 4 as the top screener, and 2 and 5 play the two-man game.

Ball Reversal to the Double Screen

If the two-man game produces no shot, 2 relays to 1, 5 moves to the bottom of the screen, waits for 1 to create a proper

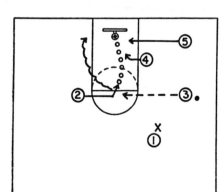

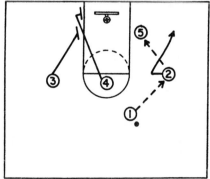

Diagram 7-21   Diagram 7-22

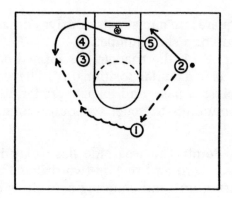

Diagram 7-23

passing angle and breaks behind the double screen for a shot or a drive opportunity. Upon passing, player 2 moves to the low-post block and rebounds a shot or awaits the counteroptions (Diagram 7-23). Refer to Chapter 4 for detailed explanation of double screen options.

Coaching Point: Even though the two-man game is an excellent option, you must instruct the strongside wing to disregard the play occasionally and immediately return the ball to the point shooter. This "automatic" action will ensure that the additional options and counteroptions will be explored.

The Guard Clearout Series Variation

The guard clearout series variation is a complete continuity pattern that successfully probes and attacks man-to-man and zone defenses. This 1-3-1 offense is unique in that it is initiated from a 2-3 formation but quickly converts to the standard tandem post options.

The play options have been previously explained and diagramed. However, it is the manner of combining these plays in a continuity pattern that ensures a smooth flowing power package.

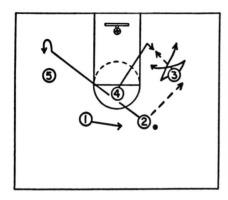

| **Diagram 7-24** | **Diagram 7-25** |

The Two-Man Game Option

Either guard may lead in to the wing on his side. Diagram 7-24 shows 2 passing to 3 and "clearing" away to the weak side baseline corner. This clearout sets up a two-man game between 3 and 4.

The Sideline Triangle Options

If 3 returns the ball to 1, 1 hits 5 and the triangle options are probed. The weakside wing stations himself at the "elbow" and may "flash" if practical (Diagram 7-25).

If necessary, the ball is passed out to the point who now joins with 3 in executing the elbow counter maneuvers: the give-and-go pick and roll, and the fake and turn. (Refer to Chapter 4, Diagrams 4-9 and 4-10.)

Coaching Point: The initial guard clearout into the weak-side triangle is an excellent zone breaker if executed as an *automatic* option. In other words, the two-man game is disregarded, and the ball is quickly reversed from wing to point to wing to baseline corner. This "quickie" movement invariably produces a good shot, not only for the corner man but also for the wing, the low post, and the weak-wing "flasher" (Diagram 7-26).

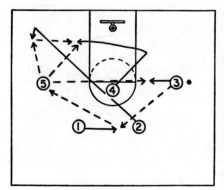

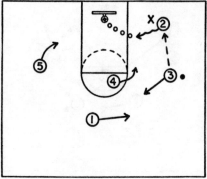

Diagram 7-26   Diagram 7-27

The Baseline "Runner" Variation

The baseline "runner" variation is a slide along the baseline from one side to the other as the ball swings. The "runner" may operate from any of three baseline spots:

1. He may set up at the strongside low post;
2. He may set up half way between the low-post spot and the corner;
3. He may move to the strongside corner to set up the triangle.

Coaching Point: The half-way position is ideal for the execution of the one-dribble jump shot since the defender usually plays baseline denial defense, leaving an open area to drive into (Diagram 7-27).

After passing to 2, 3 fakes an interchange with 1 to discourage his defender from helping X2. Player 4 moves high side and looks for possible pass from 2.

Coaching Point: As the ball swings from wing to point, the baseline runner always *moves to and stops at the low-post block on his side of the court.* This all-important technique allows the baseliner to remain in position to resume one of

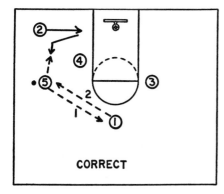

CORRECT   INCORRECT

Diagram 7-28   **Diagram 7-29**

the baseline positions quickly if the ball is returned to his side. On the other hand, if the runner continues his cut across the lane toward the other side, erroneously anticipating a quick reversal, he must reverse his direction to reach the ball side. This severely hampers the offensive objective and slows the attack (Diagrams 7-28 and 7-29).

The Inside Slice Variation

The inside slice variation began as an experiment in attacking the match-up zone. Once the rules were mastered and the continuity perfected, the "inside slice" emerged as one of our valued patterns, not only in combating the match-up but also in disrupting man and zone variations.

Again, the tandem post scoring options are the same as those previously detailed. However, since the "inside slicing" action is designed to penetrate the heart of the defense, exact timing, quick execution and precise individual fundamentals are mandatory.

The Inside Slice Rules of Action

The initial set is 1-3-1. The pattern is always initiated with a point-wing pass to the side opposite the baseline player.

The point and the high-post player perform their normal duties at their respective positions while the wings and the baseliner change sides and replace according to the following rules:

1. WINGS: "If the pass from *point to wing* or *wing to point* moves *toward* you, *hold* your position; if the pass moves *away* from you, "slice" through the "heart" of the defense, looking for the ball all the way! If you receive the pass, shoot! If you do not receive the pass, continue to one of the baseline spots on the opposite side."

2. BASELINER: "Fill the *wing* position as soon as the wing vacates ("slices"). Remember: You are now a *wing!*"

    You will note the rules in action in Diagrams 7-30 and 7-31. In Diagram 7-30, player 3 "slices" because the pass from point to wing moved away from him. Also notice that the baseliner replaces the "slicer" as he vacates the wing spot. The high post moves slightly toward the weak side and faces the basket.

Diagram 7-31 illustrates the "wing to point" rule: Player 2 relays to 1 and "slices"; 3 fills the wing; 1 hits 5; and play continues. The "slicer" must expect "body checking" tactics by the defenders; consequently, he must not "charge" as he moves through the "heart."

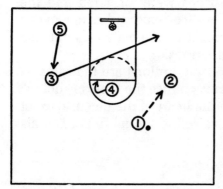

Diagram 7-30

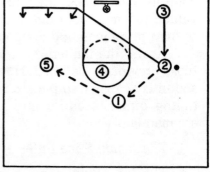

Diagram 7-31

Coaching Point: Notice that the wing, after he "slices," may elect to set up at any of the usual baseline positions: low post, halfway, or corner. The options are the same as those previously explained for those positions. Of course, the ball-handling wing must make every effort to pass to the "slicer" as soon as he "opens" in the "heart" of the defense. The "slicer" will be open for only a split second, but that is all that is needed to receive a pass, turn and shoot. Obviously, the receiver must be adept at performing the "square up" and the quick jump shot. In addition, since the defensive man on the high post usually sags back to check the "slicer," the high post is frequently open for a 15-footer. Our players not only score field goals on the heart options but also receive many free-throw attempts.

The "inside slice" is a power game! Therefore, we rebound all four of the inside players with the point remaining back as safety.

The "Right Back" Play

As you teach the "inside slice" continuity, one of the most effective moves must be emphasized. We call it the "right back." In Diagram 7-32, player 2 has the ball, 3 has "sliced"

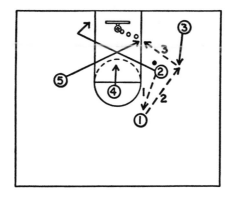

Diagram 7-32

to the baseline, and 5 has filled the wing. Player 2 passes to 1 and "slices"; however, 1, instead of swinging the ball to the other side, passes "right back" to 3 who has filled, and 5 "slices" through the "heart." This quick "crossing" pattern by the wings produces many good shot opportunities.

SUMMARY

The tandem post variations emphasized in this chapter will afford you the opportunity to add considerable power to your 1-3-1 attack. Some of the variations are designed to attack man-to-man defenses; some will produce high-percentage shots versus the zones and matchups; a few of the patterns will successfully defeat any defense.

The outside interchange, the wing-under, the high-post reverse and step-out, and the baseline exchanges are easy to teach and quickly installed. On the other hand, perfecting the up-pick, the clearout, the double screen, and the inside slice patterns will require a more concerted teaching program.

You will find that the triangle variations, the two-man game setups and the weakside flash options are "sure-fire" shot producers.

In addition to the variations explained in this chapter, we have also successfully incorporated "parts" of our other power pattern offenses: The double rotation of the posts (Chapter 3); the high-post double-screen pick-and-roll play (Chapter 4); as well as others. The resourceful coach will invent many of his own.

In short, one of these variations may be just the "edge" you are looking for!

8

Producing
High-Percentage Shots
with the Interchange-Action
Continuity Pattern

THE INTERCHANGE-ACTION CONTINUITY PATTERN

This pattern was originally intended to be a "deep-freeze" offense used to protect a lead and to run out the clock during the waning minutes of a closely contested game. However, we discovered that the constant interchanging and cutting movements performed by all five players occupied the defenders to such a degree that the basket area was frequently open for uncontested lay-ups and other types of high-percentage shots.

Consequently, the interchange-action continuity is now one of our most potent offensive weapons—not only near the end of a close contest but also at other times during the course of a game.

Note: The basic continuities are more efficiently taught and learned by establishing the *lay-up shot* as the principal objective; therefore, do not permit other types of shot opportunities during the initial stages of development of the offense—even though they are frequently available. After the basics have been established, incorporate the short jump shot, the one-on-one maneuvers and the offensive rebound attempts.

Of course, the game situation determines the tactic to be employed.

The interchange-action game is most effective against an opponent who is using an aggressive man-to-man defense. If you wish to cause the defense to change from a "packed back" zone or from a sagging man-to-man defense, the "guard-guard weakside interchange" phase of the continuity often accomplishes this objective.

Initial Set and Alignment

The offensive set is a high-and-wide 2-3 formation. The 1 and 2 positions are termed "guard spots" and are aligned approximately twelve feet apart and three feet above the top of the foul circle. The 3 and 4 positions are termed "forward spots" and align on the foul line extended and at a point approximately six feet from the sidelines. The 5 position is termed the "high post" and is initially stationed in the upper half of the foul circle (Diagram 8-1).

The perimeter spots (1-2-3-4) may be filled by either guards or forwards and the 5 spot is ideally manned by the offensive center, provided that he is capable of handling the duties of that position. (Substitutions may be necessary to ensure that players with the specific skills necessary for maximum per-

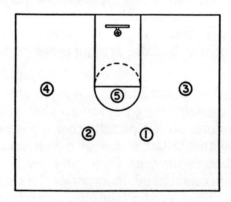

Diagram 8-1

formance are in the game when the interchange-action is employed.)

Duties and Capabilities of Players

The individual player skills necessary for maximum success are as follows: All perimeter players must be able to handle the ball, pass crisply and accurately to an open cutter, execute cuts rapidly with good body control, dribble both right- and left-handed, and shoot lay-ups accurately. The high-post player must be adept at catching the basketball, executing quick back-door cuts to the basket when appropriate, passing accurately to open cutters, and scoring on lay-ups. If he possesses a good quick fake and drive move to the basket, so much the better.

THE FOUR PHASES OF THE CONTINUITY

Phase 1:
The Guard-Guard Weak-Side Interchange

If the defense is "packed back" (tight zone defense or sagging man-to-man), begin the guard-guard interchange action immediately. This action usually prompts the defense to play more aggressively—which is just what you want to happen! As you will notice in Diagrams 8-2 and 8-3, the guard-guard interchange action is merely the execution of a guard-to-guard pass with the passer interchanging with the forward on his side of the court.

In Diagram 8-2, 2 passes to 1 and interchanges with the forward, 4, on the same side. In Diagram 8-3, 1 hits 4 coming sharply to the ball, and 1 interchanges with the forward, 3, on his side. (Notice that the left-side players always operate on the left, and right-side players always operate on the right—ideal if you have two qualified left-handers and two competent right-handers.)

Diagrams 8-4 and 8-5 show the continuity. Notice in Diagram 8-5 that after four passes and exchanges, each player is in his original starting spot.

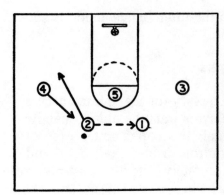

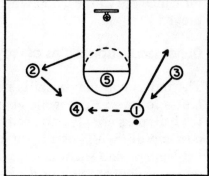

Diagram 8-2   Diagram 8-3

Coaching Point: The guard-guard interchange continuity is taught in a four-on-zero drill. Instruct the players to pass guard-guard and interchange on the weak side. Stress the 12-foot spacing. If the gap between the guard spots becomes wider than 12 feet, the danger of interception by the defense is increased. This drill is a great conditioner as well as a fine ball-handling and cutting drill. In addition, emphasize to the weak-side interchangers that the player coming down from the guard spot must *always* move to the *inside* of the forward spot interchanger, and that the guard interchanger must *always* move to the *outside*. Also stress that the guard interchanger

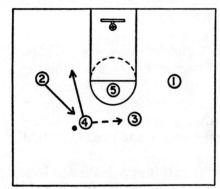

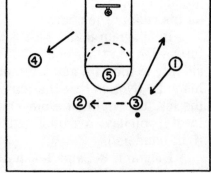

Diagram 8-4   Diagram 8-5

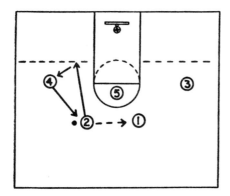

Diagram 8-6

should *never* screen for the forward. To screen on this maneuver slows the interchange and could result in costly fouls by the "screener." After the players have mastered the continuity, timing, and spacing, we add defenders and practice against defensive pressure. (This four-on-four phase also offers the defenders the opportunity to perfect the techniques of ball-side and help-side defense as well as the all-important fundamentals of "ball-you-man" defense on the cutters.) Caution the interchanger coming down from the guard spot that he is *not* to move lower than the bottom of the foul circle extended. This is important because the interchanger must immediately cut back to the forward spot to ensure a quick and efficient continuity (see Diagram 8-6).

Phase 2:
The Give-and-Go Continuity (Lay-up Time!)

When the defenders on the guard spots are playing the guard-guard passing lanes very aggressively, the cutting lanes between the high-post and the forward spots are clear all the way to the basket. The time is now right for the guard-forward give-and-go. The ball is passed from guard to forward and the passing guard fakes in the opposite direction of his pass and attempts to "rub off" his defender on the high post, who has

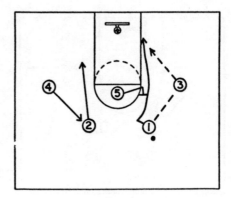

Diagram 8-7

moved to a spot just above the junction of the lane line and the foul line (Diagram 8-7).

Notice that the weakside interchange rule is still in effect as the weakside guard and forward interchange to prevent the weakside defenders from sagging back to help on the strong-side cutter.

If the cutter is *ahead* of the defender—and *only* if he is ahead—the player in the forward spot passes to him for a lay-up. (We shoot only *lay-ups*—no short jump shots, etc.) If the shot is missed and the offense gains possession, *no further shots are attempted!* The ball is returned to the guard spot and the offense resets and resumes the interchange action continuity until another lay-up opportunity results. Remember that any perimeter player may fill any outside spot on the reset.

Coaching Point: Stress the fact that cutters must precede their cuts with a long, strong step fake in the opposite direction of the cut. The cutters must *sprint* to the basket! They must keep the ball in vision at all times. (Players have a tendency to slow up after a few unsuccessful cuts to the basket. Strict emphasis on fast cuts during practice sessions will ensure proper cuts during games!) Also important is the play of the high post. First, he must set a stationary screen directly facing the direction of the cut. He *must not move* once the screen is set as this may result in a moving screen which is a foul.

Second, as the cutter from the guard spot moves past him on the cut, the high post must execute a standard pick-and-roll move to help the cutter beat his defender to the basket and to set up the next continuity option. (Do not attempt to pass the ball to the high post on his pick-and-roll move. You want this move to be only one or two short shuffle steps down the edge of the foul lane. To move him all the way down the lane would close out the basket area for the cutter and would slow the continuity.)

The continuity develops as the forward (3 in Diagram 8-8) passes to the high post as he steps back up the lane and toward the forward spot.

After passing to the high post, 3 replaces 1 at the open guard spot and 1, having been unsuccessful on his cut to the basket, moves out to the forward spot vacated by 3. The high post now passes out to either guard spot and the formation is reset and the action continues (Diagram 8-9).

If for any reason the forward cannot pass the ball to the high post, the forward dribbles out to the vacant guard spot to reset the alignment. Therefore, it is very important that the forward "saves" his dribble! (See Diagram 8-10).

After the ball has been reestablished at the guard spot, the high post moves to the middle of the foul circle and readies himself to screen again in the event of a give-and-go cut.

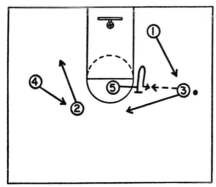

Diagram 8-8

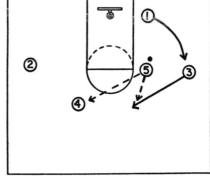

Diagram 8-9

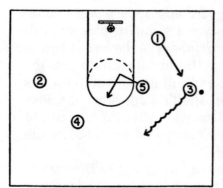

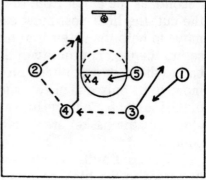

Diagram 8-10   Diagram 8-11

Coaching Point: On occasion, the guard-forward give-and-go develops so quickly that the high post is unable to move to the desired screening position. When this condition occurs, the guard cutter goes "solo." In other words, he does not wait for the screen but rather attempts to fake the defender and outrace him to the basket (Diagram 8-11).

Phase 3:
The Reverse (Backdoor) Cut Option

After the guard-guard interchange and the give-and-go cuts have been run a few times, the defense will usually attempt to cut off all passing lanes by establishing a full denial position on all potential receivers. When this defensive tactic is employed, the players begin to incorporate Phase 3, the reverse cut options, into the continuity. You will find that the high-post backdoor option and the forward reverse option will frequently provide open lay-ups.

The High-Post Backdoor Option

The high-post backdoor option is set up by the continuity move explained in Diagram 8-8, the pass from the forward to the high post. Since this forward-to-high-post pass has been completed a few times in the course of the continuity, the

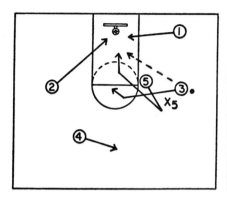

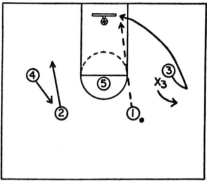

Diagram 8-12   **Diagram 8-13**

defender on the high post will attempt to deny the pass to the high post. The forward will now fake a pass to the high post and the high post will backdoor the defender and go to the basket for a lead pass and an easy score (Diagram 8-12). Note that 2, 1, and 5 rebound the shot, 3 rebounds long, and 4 is the safety.

The Forward Reverse Option

The forward reverse option is set up by the severe over-play by the forward spot defender. With the guard in control of the ball, he executes a strong ball fake to the forward. The forward takes a step to the ball as if to free himself from the defender. As the defender moves in front of the forward (between the ball and the receiver), the forward reverses direction and "explodes" to the basket. The guard either lobs the ball or executes a bounce pass to the reversing forward for a lay-up (see Diagram 8-13).

Phase 4:
The Guard High-Post Double-Cut Options

The guard High-post Double-Cut option is keyed by a direct pass from either guard spot to the high-post player. With the high post in control of the ball, *both* guards execute a quick

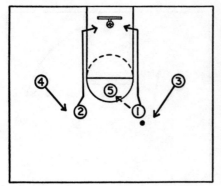

Diagram 8-14 *(Double Cut)*

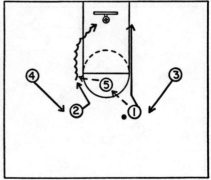

Diagram 8-15 *(Hit early)*

fake to the inside and sprint down the lane on either side of
the post man, maintaining "inside" vision on the ball as they
cut. The post man may pass to either guard providing that they
are *ahead* of their defenders. You will find that the guard
cutters may "open" either "early" or "late." If there is sufficient
distance between the post and the guard spot for the guard to
beat his defender, he may open "early" and receive a short
"float pass" from the post. In this eventuality, the guard will
speed-dribble to the basket for a lay-up (Diagrams 8-14 and 8-
15).

Should either guard be unable to clear himself "early,"

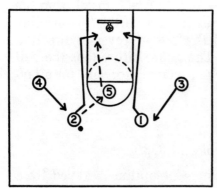

Diagram 8-16 *(Hit late)*

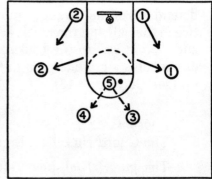

Diagram 8-17 *(Reset)*

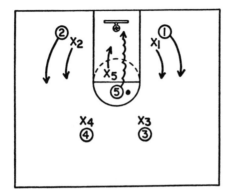

Diagram 8-18

they continue their cuts, and the high post turns, faces the basket, and watches for the opportunity to "hit them late." Often the "late" pass is the better option, particularly if the defenders on the cutters relax momentarily (Diagram 8-16).

If neither cutter opens for a pass, the continuity develops as the forwards have assumed the guard spots and the cutters move out to the forward spots. The high post returns the ball to either guard spot and the formation is again reset (Diagram 8-17).

Coaching Point: The high post is in an excellent position *to fake and drive to the basket* for a lay-up after the cutters begin their move away from the basket on their way to the forward spots. If you have confidence in the post man's ability to make this move occasionally, allow him to do so. However, it is a gamble that may backfire. Most post men, given the opportunity to do it once in awhile, will be tempted to try it too often (see Diagram 8-18).

PERFECTING THE INTERCHANGE-ACTION CONTINUITY

The teaching of the interchange-action continuity is accomplished by breakdown drills and by controlled scrimmage sessions.

1. The four-on-zero drill, explained earlier in the chapter, is very effective in establishing the cutting routes, the timing of the interchanges and the spacing. It is a great conditioner, providing that one group of four is allowed to continue for two minutes without relief (Diagrams 8-2, 8-3, 8-4, 8-5).

2. The give-and-go phase lends itself well to a simple two-on-zero drill utilizing a guard line and a forward line on both sides of the court. Guard 1 hits 2, executes a change of direction cut, receives pass from 2 and scores a lay-up. Left side shoots left-handed, right side shoots right-handed. Players exchange positions (Diagram 8-19).

3. The three-man drills (guard-forward-post) are designed to stress both the continuity and the various options. Diagram 8-20 shows the guard-forward pass and the shuffle cut by the passer off the high-post screen. Ignore the first cutter, and reset the formation by executing the pass from the forward to the high post followed by the pass from the high post to the forward who has replaced the first cutter. In other words, the players perform the strongside continuity as previously explained.

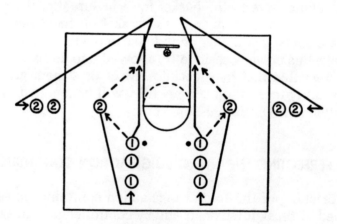

Diagram 8-19

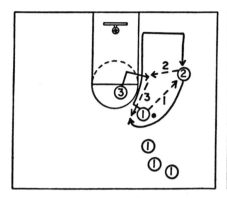 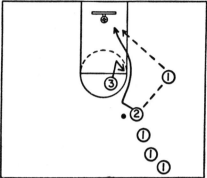

Diagram 8-20   **Diagram 8-21**

Diagram 8-21 illustrates the termination of the drill. Player 2 passes to 1 at the forward spot and shuffle cuts. 1 passes to the cutter for a lay-up. All players rebound. The players regroup, with the first cutter remaining at the forward spot, the shooter joining the guard line, and the high post remaining constant. Change post players after four repetitions.

4. As player skills increase, add the *"early"* and *"late"* scoring options, the high-post one-on-one and back-door play, the forward reverse, jump shots, and so on.

5. After the various phases have been learned via the drills, add defenders. Instruct the defenders to "make the offense look good!" In other words, ask the players to "defend" in such a way that the cutters will open occasionally, backdoor plays will work, and so on. This practice method allows the offensive players to fulfill the offensive goals. If you allow the defenders to play "lay-up prevention" defense, the offensive continuity would continue indefinitely. Naturally, you will wish to perfect the scoring options, and a "token" defense serves to make the drills enjoyable as well as profitable.

6. When the offense is working satisfactorily, five-on-five game condition drills are necessary. The offensive team is permitted to keep the ball until the defense gains control. The offense is permitted to keep the ball and reset after a score. Fouls are called and free throws are attempted.

7. Practice foul shots daily. Some coaches believe that the best way to beat the Interchange-Action game is to commit fouls and gamble that the shooter misses.

8. *Of Utmost Importance:* Make certain that you practice moving into the halfcourt pattern versus all forms of full-court pressure. When the pattern is in effect and the opponent is desperate, the full-court press will often be a part of their plan to disrupt the offense. In addition, practice the interchange-action patterns versus the various halfcourt pressure defenses, both man-to-man and zone varieties.

9. Some opponents are so concerned with protecting against the lay-up that they will station one or more defenders in the basket area and "chase" the ball with the remaining defenders. When this situation occurs, continue the continuity and play "keep-away" until the defense is forced to employ an aggressive man-to-man defense—then attack!

10. After the basic continuities and lay-up options have been mastered, add the jump shots, the clearout and the offensive rebounding attempts.

INCORPORATING THE JUMP SHOTS, THE CLEAROUT, AND THE OFFENSIVE REBOUND ATTEMPTS

The four teaching phases of the interchange-action continuity pattern have stressed lay-up shooting exclusively. When game conditions require efficient ball control and strict shot selection, the players are instructed to continue the continuity until a lay-up opportunity occurs.

The continuity is equally effective as a "high-scoring"

offense, and we frequently employ it as such by adding the *jump shot, a clearout option,* and *the offensive rebound attempts.*

For example, the high-post fake and drive option explained in Diagram 8-18 is now encouraged. The one-dribble jump shot is usually open if the lay-up is not.

You also will discover that the guard-high post double cut option is an excellent jump-shot producer, particularly as the guard cutters begin their moves out to the forward spots to reset the formation (Diagram 8-17). The defenders on the cutters, having successfully denied the "hit late" option (Diagram 8-16), have a tendency to relax their defense on the cutters as they move away from the basket. The high-post player passes to the "hooking" cutter who shoots a quick jump shot or executes a drive to the basket.

We also add a simple guard clearout option. In this maneuver we signal the option with a guard-forward pass, after which the passing guard, instead of executing the usual give-and-go cut, clears to the weak side. This clearing action allows the forward the opportunity to beat his defender one-on-one or play the two-man game with the post player.

Finally, we now attack the offensive backboard with the intention of scoring a field goal or drawing a foul by the defense. (In the lay-up only game, we do not attempt to score on offensive rebounds since the probability of loss of ball possession is great.)

SUMMARY

You will find the interchange-action continuity pattern to be effective not only as a *lay-up game* but also as a *high-percentage shot producer.* The constant player movements, the quick cuts to the basket, and the backdoor scoring thrusts blend perfectly with the floor balancing continuity.

Each of the four phases of the offense is readily adaptable to efficient breakdown drills. These drills will provide the coach with a sound and practical method of establishing and teaching the fundamentals and techniques necessary to the efficient execution of the offense. In addition, the incorporation of the other high-percentage shot options will greatly enhance the point-scoring potential.

You also will discover that the best testimonial to the effectiveness of the interchange-action continuity will come from the players on your squad who have to defend against it in practice sessions. To defend against it will become one of their most detestable chores.

After many years of use, the interchange-action is still one of our favorite techniques. It has been directly responsible for many of our victories. I am convinced that the pattern will prove to be as successful for your team as it has been for the many coaches who have included the interchange-action continuity pattern in their offensive repertoire!

9

Scoring Easy Baskets with the Endline, Sideline, Jump-Ball, and Delay Power Patterns

SPECIAL SITUATION PLAYS

These plays provide the well-prepared team with quick and effective scoring opportunities. Endline plays are designed to attack the straight zone sets and the man-to-man defenses; sideline plays take advantage of defenses that are drilled to deny the in-bounds pass; jump-ball or tap formations serve as ideal "springboards" for a fast-break thrust or for a set play; and well-conceived and executed "delay" patterns not only eat up the clock but also open the basket area for easy lay-up scores.

Since these special situation plays provide made-to-order opportunities for quick and easy scores, we regard these plays to be as important as any other part of our offensive systems.

Each of the special situation plays includes maneuvers and options that are integral parts of established patterns. Consequently, a minimum of additional learning time is required in order to achieve perfection.

PERFECTING THE ENDLINE PLAYS

Because the vast majority of teams have shifted to the zone defense as a "stopper" for under-the-basket out-of-bounds plays, we reluctantly scrapped our favorite man-to-man plays in favor of the all-purpose attack principle. Fortunately, this decision proved to be a blessing in disguise! After a few experimental practice sessions, we devised three multioption endline attacks that have proved to be vastly more productive than any of our former plays. We have termed them the "Big Three": "Ohio," "Texas," and "Utah."

Scoring with "Ohio"

The initial player positioning is shown in Diagram 9-1.

Player Capabilities and Requirements

Player 1, the inbounder, must be a capable passer and a good medium-distance jump shooter. Player 2 is usually a guard; he is primarily a feeder. Player 3 must also possess an accurate outside shot. Player 4 is a primary rebounder, a screener, and must be able to post up and play the two-man game on occasion. Player 5 should be a tall player, since he always moves to the basket for a high pass as the first option of the play.

Of course, the above requirements are ideal; however, players of average height and ability also can work wonders from this formation!

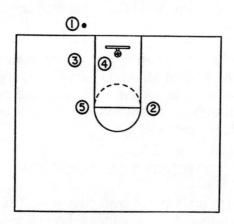

Diagram 9-1

First Phase Options

In Diagram 9-2, player 1 initiates the action as the official hands him the ball, 3 spreads toward the baseline corner, 4 moves toward the weak side of the basket, 5 breaks to the basket on the strong side, 2 replaces 5.

The first option is the pass to player 5 for the power lay-up or the short jumper. Player 1 also looks for 4, who is frequently open for a lay-up and a possible three-point play. If 3 receives 1's pass, he can shoot, hit 5 posting low, or relay to 2 who has moved into 17-foot shooting range. Of course, 1 may pass directly to 2. Player 2 is the safety and the others rebound. If either 4 or 5 receives the inbounds pass, the shot is immediate (Diagram 9-3). Notice that 1 moves to the weak side after inbounding the ball.

Second Phase Options

If neither 2 nor 3 is open for a good shot, or if 3 cannot hit 5 on the low post, the second phase of "Ohio" is implemented. Player 3 passes to 2 and 5 sprints to the weakside guard spot. Player 2 relays to 5, who may hit 1 or 4 who "begs" for the ball after 1 has "popped." Players 1 and 4 have the option of shooting or playing the two-man game. If the inbounds pass goes directly from 1 to 2, the same continuity results. Player 2 is safety; all others rebound (Diagram 9-4).

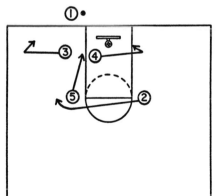

Diagram 9-2

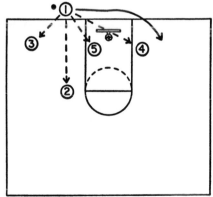

Diagram 9-3

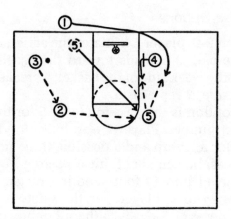

Diagram 9-4

Coaching Point: This "play" is really a complete pattern offense initiated from the baseline rather than from the usual guard spots. Our opponents know this play as well as we do; stopping it is another matter! The main concern for the defense is "clogging" 5's initial thrust to the basket. This tactic tends to free the other players for an open shot.

Countering with "Texas"

Like "Ohio," "Texas" is also a multioption continuity offense. The initial set is exactly the same; however, some effective counterplays are incorporated in both the first and second phases of the play.

First-Phase Options

In Diagram 9-5, the "Ohio" cuts have been completed, and neither 5 nor 4 has "opened." Player 1 passes to 3 and cuts toward the weak side as usual. Player 3 relays to 2, joins 5 in a double screen, and 1 counters by coming back around the double screen, receives the pass from 2, and shoots. Again, 2 is safety and 1, 3, 4, and 5 rebound.

Second-Phase Options

If 1 cannot shoot, a drive into the packed defense is not practical; consequently, 1 passes to 2, triggering the second

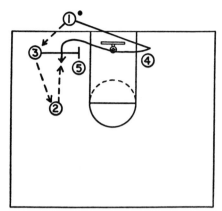
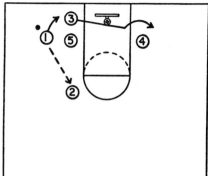

Diagram 9-5   Diagram 9-6

phase. After 1 relays to 2, 1 cuts to the baseline side of 5; 3 moves across the lane to the baseline side of 4 (Diagram 9-6).

Diagram 9-7 illustrates the second-phase scoring options. Player 2 immediately looks for 3 popping out from behind 4's screen. If 3 is not open, 2 looks for 1 popping out from behind 5's pick. Again, the receivers may shoot or play the two-man game.

Coaching Point: The "Texas" continuity is particularly effective as a short outside attack against the defense that *absolutely refuses* to give up the inside shot and remains packed in the lane area. It also becomes apparent that players 1 and

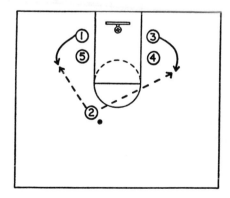

Diagram 9-7

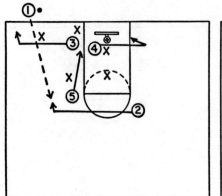 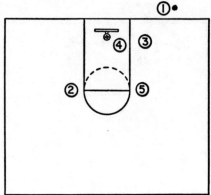

Diagram 9-8   **Diagram 9-9**

3 must be your best shooters, as they are the recipients of most of the outside opportunities.

The "Ohio" and the "Texas" plays complement one another perfectly. *However, there is one adjustment that must be made when the inbounds spot is near the baseline corner.* Since 3 will not have enough space in which to maneuver for the inbounds pass, the pass must go directly to 2, who will then initiate the second-phase action. Naturally, if 5 or 4 is open, 1 will hit the open player (Diagram 9-8).

Finally, the initial alignment of "Ohio" and "Texas" is the same regardless of the inbounding side (Diagram 9-9).

Changing Pace with the "Utah" Quickie Play

The "Utah" play is designed to produce a quick, high-percentage shot when time does not permit the continuity approach. In addition, this single-action play provides a change of pace from our normal "Ohio" and "Texas" patterns.

The "Utah" formation is the familiar foul-line four-in-line set. Player 1 inbounds as usual, but 2, 3, 4, and 5 align as shown in Diagram 9-10.

"Utah" Scoring Options

Player 1 inbounds the ball; 3 steps around 2's screen and slashes toward the ball; 2 breaks to corner as 3 cuts by. On the

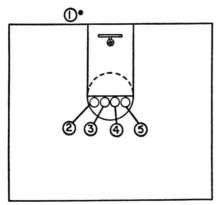

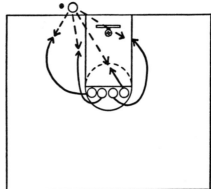

Diagram 9-10   Diagram 9-11

opposite side of the line, 4 breaks around 5 and 5 steps toward the ball. Player 1 can inbound to any of the three cutters or feed 5 in the lane. The feed to 5 is frequently the best option while the defense is concentrating on the three cutters. This play spreads the defense and often produces a high-percentage shot with a minimum of ball movement. Player 5 should be a tall player and must act as the defensive balance. The other four rebound. If the inbounder sets on the other side, all positions are reversed (see Diagram 9-11).

Coaching Points: The inbounder must "signal" the play before taking the ball from the official, preferably before assuming his inbounding position. This necessary technique allows the players to move into the proper formation and "mentally adjust" to the play. To call the name of the play, "Ohio," "Texas," "Utah," and so on, would tend to alert the defense; therefore, we teach the following signal system: "Ohio" is number 1, 2, or 3; "Texas" is number 4, 5, or 6; "Utah" is number 7, 8, or 9. The inbounder always calls the play orally. In addition, some game situations call for caution; that is, we may prefer to control the ball rather to attempt to score. If this is the case, the inbounder calls the number 10 or the word "first" and the "Ohio" cuts proceed as usual; however, the inbounder's first option is to pass the ball over the defense to 2 who breaks toward the midcourt line. If another player receives the ball, no shot is attempted, the formation resets, and the strategy in effect at this time continues. This plan allows the coach to relay manual or verbal signals from the bench.

INITIATING THE "MAINE" SIDELINE
OUT-OF-BOUNDS ATTACKS VERSUS PRESSURE

The sideline plays are designed to ensure safe inbounding and to score lay-ups versus the aggressive man-to-man defenses. The three sideline patterns are termed Maine "Zero," Maine "One," and Maine "Two." The initial formations of each pattern are shown in Diagrams 9-12a, b, and c.

The terms "Zero," "One," and "Two" refer to the number of players initially positioned ahead of the ball. If the inboun-

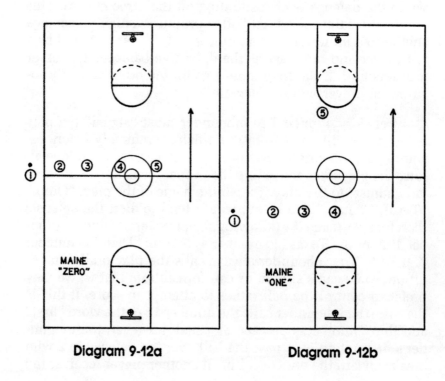

Diagram 9-12a   Diagram 9-12b

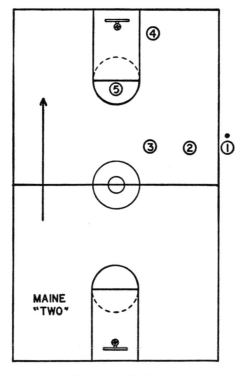

Diagram 9-12c

der calls Maine "Zero," players 2, 3, 4, and 5 align in single file, approximately six feet apart, and face the inbounder. In other words, "Zero" players "ahead of the ball," as illustrated in Diagram 9-12a.

The inbounder's call of "One" keys the formation shown in Diagram 9-12b—"one" player "ahead of the ball." Likewise, the call of "Two" alerts designated players 4 and 5 to set "ahead of the ball" as shown in Diagram 9-12c.

The options peculiar to each formation are effective from any sideline inbounding spot, providing that the defense is aggressively overplaying the passing lanes. Safe inbounding leads to 2 and 3 are usually available, and proper execution of fakes, screens, "backdoor" maneuvers, and direct basket cuts by players 1, 4, and 5 frequently result in lay-up opportunities.

Scoring with Maine "Zero"

At the first indication of sideline pressure by the defense, we set up Maine "Zero." The player in the 5 spot is ideally fast, sure-handed, and a capable lay-up shooter. Player 1 must be proficient at completing the lead pass to 5 breaking to the basket, to 2 or 3 cutting to the rear, or to 4 moving straight toward the ball.

In Diagram 9-13, the defense is pressuring in a straight man-to-man. As the inbounder receives the ball, 2 breaks back short, and 3 breaks back long in order to create two passing openings. Player 4 turns, faces his basket and holds, setting a wide screen. Player 5 fakes two or three steps back, "rubs" off 4's screen, and flies to the hoop, looking for a lead pass from 1. Player 4 moves toward the inbounder in a straight line after

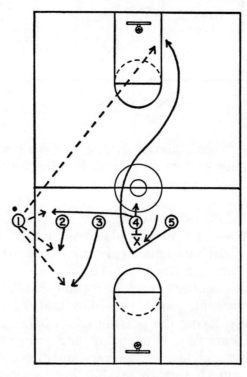

Diagram 9-13

5 moves past. Player 1's first option is to hit 5 for the lay-up. Players 2, 3, and 4 are safe inbounding choices.

Countering with Maine "One"

Maine "Zero" usually produces a lay-up if all five defenders are "tight." However, the defender, having been "burned" once, sensibly counters by shifting toward the basket to prevent the lay-up. The offense also counters by positioning a capable post player ahead of the ball and initiating Maine "One," a highly successful give-and-go play with a backdoor option.

In Diagram 9-14, a predesignated post player has shaped up at the top of the key since the ball is being inbounded at a mid-backcourt spot. Player 1 observes post player 4's defender and executes the appropriate play: If the defender has assumed

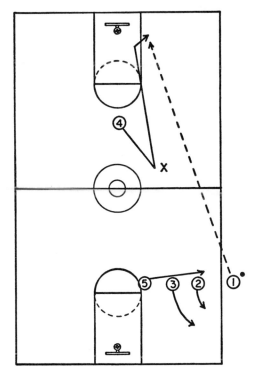

Diagram 9-14

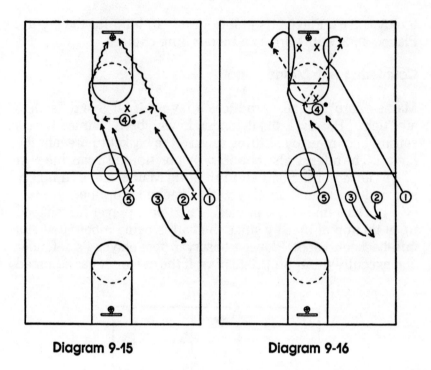

Diagram 9-15   Diagram 9-16

a front denial position, 1 performs a good ball fake, 4 takes
one long step toward the ball, and reverses to the basket for a
lob pass and a backdoor lay-up.

On the other hand, if the defender is playing behind or
slightly to one side of 4, 4 breaks toward the ball, receives 1's
pass, and 1 and 5 sprint down their respective sides. If either
cutter is ahead of his defender, 4 passes for a lay-up. (Diagram
9-15.)

If neither cutter opens, 4 faces the basket and may drive
or hit 1 or 5 with a "late" pass as they "flare." Players 1, 4,
and 5 rebound; 2 and 3 trail the play (Diagram 9-16).

Implementing Maine "Two"

Another successful sideline variation, Maine "Two," positions
two players ahead of the ball, usually the center and a forward.

This formation has proved to be a terrific scoring pattern at any inbounding point along the sideline, and particularly as an attack to defeat the popular frontcourt-sideline presses.

In Diagram 9-17a, 1 is the inbounder and 2 and 3 align as usual. Forward 4 sets at the low-post block and center 5 shapes up at the high-post position. As 1 receives the ball, 2 and 3 cut back as always; 4 and 5 break toward the ball and the defense "names the play."

The various options of Maine "Two" depend on the reactions of defenders X4 and X5 as 4 and 5 break toward the ball:

1. If both defenders front the cut, both 4 and 5 reverse to the basket following the usual ball fake cue by 1. Player 1 lobs to either 4 or 5 (Diagram 9-17b).

2. If one back defender "fronts" and the other plays behind

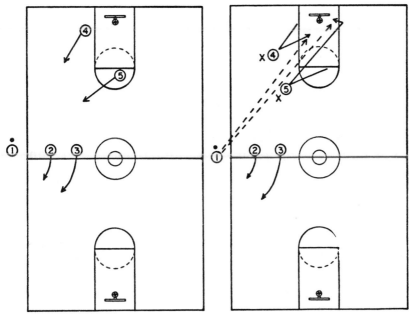

Diagram 9-17a   Diagram 9-17b

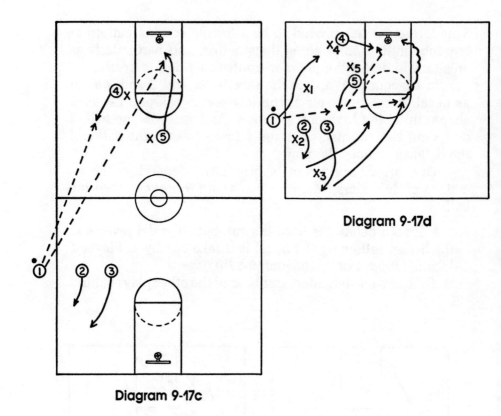

Diagram 9-17d

Diagram 9-17c

or to one side, 1 has two options: He may fake the pass and lob to the "fronted" player, or he may pass to the other player as he advances to the ball (Diagram 9-17c).

3. If 1 passes to 5, the advancing cutter, 5 may feed 4 on the "backdoor" cut or hit 3 sprinting down the weak side. Player 1 cuts to the outside of 4; 3, 4, and 5 rebound; 2 is safety (Diagram 9-17d).

4. If 5 is overplayed and 4 is open on his advance, 4 can hit 5 on the "backdoor" cut, 3 continues to the basket as a rebounder and 1 cuts outside of 4 for a possible pass and shot. Notice that when the ball is inbounded at a sideline spot close to the endline, players 2 and 3 do not have enough open space to perform their usual back cuts. In this situation, 2 screens for 3 and rolls back to the ball as 3 "rubs off" the screen (Diagram 9-17e).

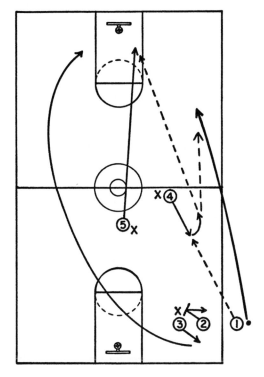

Diagram 9-17e

Coaching Points: The fake pass that triggers the backdoor play is vital to the success of this lay-up producing maneuver. First, the fake serves as a signal to the receiver that the play is on. Second, the fake "tells" the receiver that he must step strongly to the ball before he reverses to the basket. This fake by the passer and the subsequent step by the receiver perfectly sets up the defender for the backdoor cut.

Furthermore, the distances between the inbounder and the downcourt receiver(s) in the Maine "One" and "Two" plays must be consistent. For example, the positioning distances in Diagram 9-17a are ideal for an inbounding play from the midcourt line. Various inbounding positions in the *backcourt* require the player or players who are "ahead of the ball" to adjust their setup positions accordingly. (Refer to Diagrams 9-17 c, d, and e for examples of position adjustment.)

The three Maine sideline attacks will enable you to disrupt the aggressive sideline denial tactics of the pressure defenses—and score lay-ups in the process!

IMPLEMENTING THE JUMP BALL OR TAP PLAYS

The recent "alternating out-of-bounds rule" enacted by the National Federation Basketball Rules Committee has eliminated all jump ball situations except at the beginning of the game and at the start of each overtime period. However, the center-circle tap play, properly executed, affords an excellent opportunity for a great beginning, whether it occurs at the opening tip-off or at the beginning of a crucial overtime period.

Our primary objective is to attack with the early-offense transition patterns, as detailed in Chapter 1. Both the 2-1-2 and the 1-3-1 sets are ideal formations for the implementation of the early-offense patterns.

Attacking from the 2-1-2 Formation

Diagram 9-18a shows the initial 2-1-2 formation, which is basically the same as the 2-1-2 defensive formations illustrated in Chapter 1, Diagrams 1-3a and 1-3b. Player 5 is our best "jumper", 1 and 2 the front line "breakers", 3 fills the open lane, and 4 is a trailer. Player 5, after successfully directing the tap, also trails. (The jumper always "delays" before entering the center-circle in order to allow his teammates the opportunity to observe the positioning of the defenders.)

Coaching Point: The 2-1-2 formation is not only ideal for starting the early-offense patterns, it also provides excellent defensive balance should you fail to gain possession on the tap. Always employ this formation when you are not sure about controlling the tap.

Diagram 9-18b shows 1 receiving the tap, passing to 2 in the middle, 3 filling the open lane, and 4 and 5 trailing. If the tap goes to 2, 1 fills the middle, 3 cuts in a straight line to the open wing, and 4 and 5 trail as usual (Diagram 9-18c).

If the front receiver is unable to pass to the middle man,

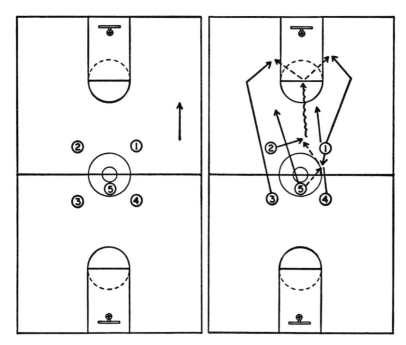

Diagram 9-18a   Diagram 9-18b

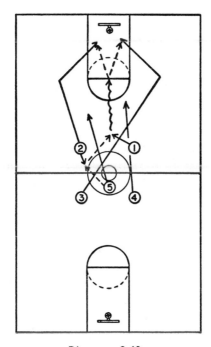

Diagram 9-18c

165

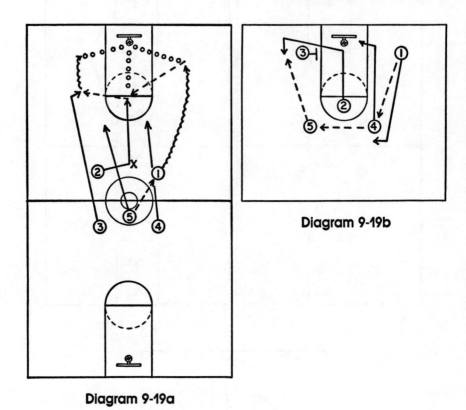

Diagram 9-19b

Diagram 9-19a

he dribbles down the sideline, looking for a Go attack scoring opportunity (Diagram 9-19a). The completion of the first swing of the Swing It phase is illustrated in Diagram 9-19b.

If none of the first swing options are open, the second swing options follow. (Refer to Chapter 1, Diagrams 1-5 through 1-11, for a complete review of the early offense swing patterns and adjustments.)

Attacking from the 1-3-1 Formation

The 1-3-1 formation is also an excellent springboard for the early offense tap attack. However, never employ the 1-3-1 formation when you are not certain that you can control the tap, since it is a weak defensive formation. In the 1-3-1 formation the wings, 2 and 3, set wide. This "wide wing" set accomplishes two important objectives:

1. If the defenders play a tight man-to-man defense, player 1 is always open for the tap because X1 must play to one side or the other, or directly behind 1. The jumper then taps away from the defender. Wings 2 and 3 fill the wings and 4 and 5 trail (Diagram 9-20).

2. Should the defenders align in a basket-protecting defense—usually a 1-1-2-1 zone formation—the "wide wing" setup assures at least one open "tapping spot." As Diagram 9-21 shows, the defense is in reality giving up possession of the ball in order to prevent an easy basket (Diagram 9-21).

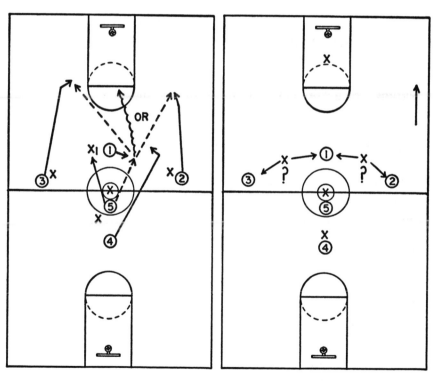

Diagram 9-20   Diagram 9-21

Naturally, the fundamentals of tapping to the open side of the receiver, meeting the tap by the receiver, and converting to the early offense attack must be stressed. However, since the tap attack is merely a special adaptation of the early offense transition patterns, a bare minimum of additional teaching is required!

Coaching Point: The early offense tap attack is ideal not only as a quick-hitting scoring play but also as a positive starting approach. Scoring a lay-up or a short jump shot by way of a precisely executed opening tap play may very well provide just the igniting spark you had hoped for!

Even though the tap play occurs only once during the course of a regulation contest, the time devoted to installing and perfecting it will be well spent.

CONTROLLING THE DEFENSE AND SCORING WITH THE TRIANGLE-AND-TWO POWER PATTERN DELAY GAME

Player Placement and Initiating the Patterns

The triangle-and-two delay pattern is a dynamite offense for teams that desire to stall for time and open the basket area for unmolested lay-up opportunities. Even those teams that are required to play under the restrictions of a shot-clock will discover that the triangle-and-two is an effective "short-time" strategy.

The triangle-and-two utilizes the three most proficient ball handlers in a center-court triangle continuity. The wide wing spots are filled by the remaining two players, usually the center and the big forward. Diagram 9-22 shows the initial traingle-and-two formation.

The guards, 1 and 2, initiate the action in one of three ways:

1. Pass to the high post;
2. Pass to the opposite guard;
3. Pass to a wide wing.

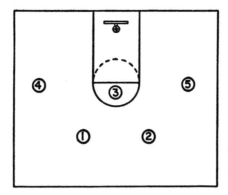

Diagram 9-22

Each initiating pass triggers a cut from a guard spot to the basket. In addition, if no lay-up materializes, the center-court triangle reforms and the continuity continues.

IMPLEMENTING THE TRIANGLE-ROTATION CONTINUITY AND SCORING OPTIONS

The Guard-High-Post Entry Option

Guard 1 hits high-post player 3, executes a change of direction cut and blasts to the basket on either side of 3. If 1 has his defender "beat," 3 passes and a lay-up results (Diagram 9-23).

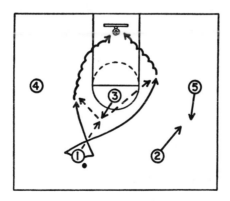

Diagram 9-23

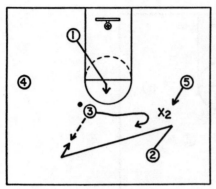

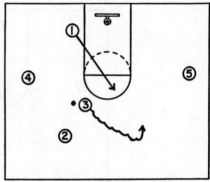

Diagram 9-24a   Diagram 9-24b

As 1 cuts to the basket, 2 fakes an interchange with 5 to prevent X2 from sagging back toward 3, then replaces 1 at the vacant guard spot. Player 3 has *two reset options:* He may pass to 2 and fill the open guard spot as 1 breaks sharply to replace him at the high post (Diagram 9-24a).

Player 3's *second option* is to dribble to the open guard position, 1 fills the high post, and the triangle reforms (Diagram 9-24b).

The Guard-Guard Entry Option

As guard 1 passes to guard 2, he cuts to either side of the high post, looking for a lead pass from 2. If no opening results, 3 replaces 1, 1 fills at the high post, and the pattern is ready to resume (Diagram 9-25).

The Guard-Wing Entry Options

The Basket Cut

When the guard passes to the wide wing, he may execute a basket cut or initiate a "guard squeeze" play. Diagram 9-26 illustrates the basket cut and the "no-shot" continuity. Player 1 passes to 4 and performs the usual change of direction cut to the basket. If 1 is unsuccessful on his cut, he replaces 3, 3 replaces 2, 2 replaces 1 and 4 passes to 2 who may initiate any one of the three entry options.

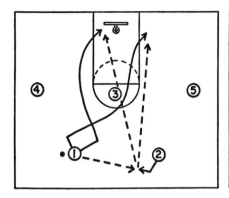

Diagram 9-25

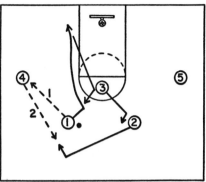

Diagram 9-26

The "Guard Squeeze" Play

If the guard elects to run the "guard squeeze" play, he passes to the strongside wide wing and sets an inside screen for the opposite guard. In Diagram 9-27a, 2 hits 5 and screens X1. Player 1 moves back one step, extends his hands toward 5 as if to ready himself to receive a pass, and 5, reading the play perfectly, fakes a pass to 1. (These faking maneuvers are designed to bring X1 "up tight" so that he can be "run into" the screen.) Player 3 also positions himself as a stationary screener, and 1 slices to the basket, using the multiple screens to free himself for a lay-up. Diagram 9-27b shows the reset continuity.

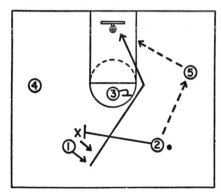

Diagram 9-27a

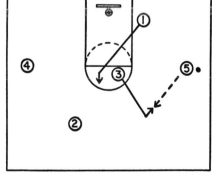

Diagram 9-27b

Special Countermaneuvers

After we score a lay-up or two, one or both defensive wings usually drop back to help the triangle defenders protect the basket area. Either guard can counter this defensive measure by passing to an open wing, and delaying the basket cut or squeeze play until the defender advances to the ball.

Another favorite defensive stunt is to sag the weakside wing defender into the lane area whenever the high post is in control of the ball. The high post counters this move by passing to the open wing. In this countermove, guard 1 has made his basket cut and 2 has replaced him. The high post, 3, passes to the open wing, replaces 2 according to the rules of the continuity, and 5 passes to 3. Player 1 fills the high-post spot and the pattern continues (Diagram 9-28).

Another sure lay-up option versus the aggressive wing defender is the guard-wing backdoor play, explained in Diagram 5-16a, Chapter 5.

In the event that one or both defenders drop off the guards to deny the pass to the high post, the guards counter by holding the ball, passing the ball between them, or initiating either of the guard-wing plays.

Note: The term *guard* used throughout the discussion of the triangle-and-two power pattern delay game refers to any

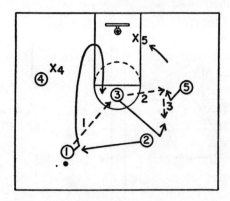

Diagram 9-28

player who performs at either guard spot as the continuity progresses. By the same token, the term high post refers to any player who performs high-post duties.

The triangle-and-two pattern is always used when we are protecting a lead during the waning minutes of a close contest. Moreover, we frequently employ the pattern against an aggressive defense at various times during a game, regardless of the time remaining. Of course, the triangle-and-two is most effective when we enjoy a lead; however, when the defense continues to use pressure tactics, we often use it successfully even when behind in the score!

Another "plus" of the triangle-and-two is that the limited action required of the wide wings (usually your big men) affords them a "breather" and minimizes their chances of fouling.

TEACHING THE TRIANGLE-AND-TWO
POWER PATTERN DELAY GAME

Begin teaching the triangle phase of the triangle-and-two via the three-on-zero progression method. Drill the players who will be used in the center-court triangle continuities. The wings should practice other appropriate fundamentals until the time is right to incorporate them into the total scheme.

The first step in the progression is to explain and walk through the guard-high post entry, stressing continuity only. Emphasize the basket cut, the change of direction move, and the crossover cut from the guard spots. Teach the two high-post reset options: the *pass and fill* and the *dribble fill.* After the continuity has been mastered, work to perfect the high-post passing techniques, the high-speed lay-up shots, and the rebound pattern. Progress to jog-through and run-through sessions, continuing to emphasize all the fine points. Finalize the progression with programmed defensive work, followed by halfcourt and fullcourt scrimmage sessions.

The same progression should be followed in teaching the guard-guard entry. Reemphasize the change of direction basket cut, the crossover cut and the reset continuity. Add the fundamentals of the *guard-to-guard lead pass* and the *receiver's lay-up shot.*

At this point in the teaching progression, practice combining the guard-high post entry with the guard-guard entry. Repeat the three-on-three continuity and option drills, the three-on-three defensive programing procedures, and the halfcourt scrimmage. Continue to emphasize that error-free execution is vital—the outcome of many games may very well depend on it!

When the guard-high post and the guard-guard entries are satisfactory, the addition of the guard-wing entry completes the halfcourt teaching progression. Incorporate the guard-wing basket cut, the guard "squeeze play," and the countermoves. Periodic drill and frequent halfcourt scrimmage will iron out the wrinkles and keep your players sharp.

Coaching Point: While the triangle-and-two power pattern delay game is a halfcourt offense, it is mandatory to practice initiating it versus the various full-court presses, since the defensive team—behind in the score and desperate—will undoubtedly launch an all-out pressure attack! Of course, after crossing the midcourt line, this pressure will be to your advantage!

SUMMARY

Special situation plays are important parts of the power pattern offensive system! The endline, sideline, jump ball, and delay patterns generate a respectable percentage of total scores—game after game!

Many coaches make the grave mistake of relegating special situation tactics to last place in their practice planning. The wise coach begins to install out-of-bounds plays, jumpball formations, and delay procedures during the first few days of practice and continues to sharpen each tactic as the season progresses.

The "Ohio," "Texas," and "Utah" endline plays are the best of the many that we have used over the years. Each play is designed to score against both zone and man-to-man defenses. In addition, each pattern provides a "safety valve" for control purposes.

The Maine "Zero," "One," and "Two" sideline attacks are easily learned and are totally effective versus sideline presses. So effective, in fact, that our players greet any form of sideline pressure with the words "lay-up time"!

The center-jump circle is a perfect "launching pad" for a tap play basket and an early edge at the beginning of a game or at the start of an overtime period.

If you are a believer in the delay offense, and the rules under which you compete make the employment of a "delay game" practical, the triangle-and-two power pattern delay game provides your players with a safe and sound system of play— not only as a delaying tactic but as a lay-up scoring attack as well! The practice of working the center-court triangle continuity and "isolating" the wings creates perplexing problems for the defense: If the defenders "pack the basket" to deny the lay-up, counter by holding the ball until they are forced by the lack-of-action rule to attempt to gain control of the ball within five seconds. On the other hand, when the defenders play aggressively, go for the lay-up! You will be thoroughly satisfied with the triangle-and-two—and so will your players!

No question about it—special situation plays, included as vital parts of your total offensive package, will provide many "bonus" baskets!

10

A Word
to the Wise:
"It's the Execution
that Counts"

Each basketball coach has his own philosophy, his own favorite style of play, his own methods of achieving objectives. Regardless of the many differences among coaches in these areas, all have the same ultimate goal—*winning!*

None of us is so naive as to believe that *our* offense system is the *only* system of play. The wise coach realizes that the total is no greater than the sum of its parts. He is firmly convinced that the teaching of sound fundamentals is absolutely necessary to the eventual success of any system—no matter what it may be! In short, the wise coach knows that *it's not the play, but the execution of the play that counts!*

Without question, our approach to the teaching of fundamentals is directly responsible for the success of the power pattern offenses. When installing a fundamental drill program, certain rules will assure satisfactory results: All drills must be functional and should teach what you want taught. Furthermore, what you want taught must always be an actual part of your offensive system. Any drill, no matter how attractive or fancy, that does not teach the exact fundamentals required in the offensive patterns should be eliminated. Time is much too precious to be wasted on irrelevant drills!

Begin each drill session by "preaching" *perfection* to your players. Inform them that each drill is designed to teach one, and only one, fundamental. For example, a ball-fake drill teaches only ball faking, a square-up drill emphasizes only squaring up; a baseball-pass drill stresses only the baseball pass!

Note: I arrived at the decision to teach *one fundamental at a time* because I discovered that one of our combination drills which combined the fundamentals of passing, dribbling, pivoting and shooting produced a player who was a "Jack of all trades and master of none!" After all, to teach one fundamental is difficult enough—to teach *four* at one time is impossible!

For this reason, never combine two or more fundamentals in a single drill until the proper execution of each fundamental is firmly established. When you are satisfied that the players have mastered the fundamentals, then combination drills should be introduced.

When the progression drills are implemented, emphasize specific points of execution:

1. Swinging the ball takes away the help-side defense.
2. When an individual defender is playing soft (sagging), move toward him; when he is playing hard (ball denial), move in the direction that he is overplaying.
3. Always pass *away* from the defense.
4. The defense *names* the play!
5. You don't have to *look*, but you must *see!*
6. Don't pick up your dribble unless you have a pass or a shot.
7. Speed, but *controlled* speed!

In addition to stressing specific points of execution as the progression drills continue, the practice of naming a shooter or demanding a certain number of passes before attempting a good shot greatly improves the ball handling and the change-of-sides continuity.

The post players should practice their short hook shots, turn-around jumpers, power moves and various footwork maneuvers in supervised one-on-one drills. When working in five-on-zero or five-on-five halfcourt drills, *the post players must master four basic fundamental options:*

1. maneuvering for the shot
2. passing to the other post (if any)
3. fanning to a weakside perimeter player
4. playing the two-man game with a strongside player

Hammer away at these all-important post options until the post players are able to execute them quickly and accurately!

You can easily invent drills for teaching the techniques of screening, cutting, flashing, posting, "begging," rebounding, and so on. Position the appropriate number of players who will be involved in a certain play situation at one or more baskets, explain what they are to accomplish, and begin the drill.

All drills must be supervised. Of course, if you are fortunate enough to have one or more assistant coaches, supervision is no problem. On the other hand, if you are the sole supervisor, coaching each drill station is difficult, but *supervision must be accomplished if the drill is to be productive!*

Since shooting the basketball is really the pay-off fundamental, perfection in this area is vital. Of course, all coaches emphasize proper shooting techniques and devote an appropriate portion of practice time to shooting drills. However, three specific shooting skills must be mastered: the quick-set shot, the pull-up jumper, and the one-dribble jump shot.

The quick-set shot is vital, particularly when attacking a zone defense. The shooter should be taught to take the pass facing the basket and with his body in a proper shooting stance. Upon receiving the ball, he must "get it away" without delay. Even when facing man-to-man defenses, a quick fan-out from the low- or high-post player will provide a perimeter player with an open shot before a sagging defender is able to recover from a helping position. If a player is unable to master the set shot, a quick jumper is permissible providing that the shot is "launched" without dribbling.

The pull-up jump shot is equally important, particularly following a rapid dribble into the scoring area. A full-court dribbling drill emphasizing a full speed dribble, a balanced stop, a quick square up and a fundamentally sound jump shot is an excellent teaching tool.

Finally, the *one-dribble jump shot* is perhaps the most devastating individual offensive weapon in the game of basketball. Combining this maneuver with jab steps, crossovers, and rocker fakes will enable a player to free himself for a great shot both inside and outside the defense. Without this move, a player is helpless in heavy defensive traffic! Mastery of this important fundamental is an *absolute necessity!*

The power pattern offenses are systems of play that consistently produce winning teams. Even though the National Rules Committees have frequently altered the rules and regulations for interscholastic and collegiate play, the power pattern offenses have survived and prospered! One "rule" that will remain forever constant is Dr. James Naismith's original objective of the game of basketball: "The object of the game is to put the ball into your opponent's goal." Teams using the power patterns have fulfilled that objective—and, I might add—more frequently than have the opponents!

Two guiding principles are largely responsible for the success that the power pattern offenses have provided: "The defense names the play," and "It's the execution that counts."

Index